Cooking Pasta with Adelina

BECAUSE LIFE IS *too* SHORT *for* PLAIN NOODLES

Adelina Willem
Ana Willem (Illustrations)

Dedication

*To my grandmother and my mother, who made sure
I learned how to cook; and to Raymond, Ana and Bel,
who gave me a reason to enjoy it.*

Cover photograph by Tonya Evatt

Published by
Adelina Willem
635 College Place
Las Cruces, New Mexico 88005
(505) 524-3459

Copyright© Adelina Willem

Library of Congress Number: 95-61898
ISBN: 0-9648810-0-4

Designed, Edited, and Manufactured by
Favorite Recipes® Press
P.O. Box 305142
Nashville, Tennessee 37230
1-800-358-0560

Manufactured in the United States of America
First Printing: 1995   5,000 copies
Second Printing: 1996   5,000 copies

Acknowledgments

he concept of this book as a tool for learning to cook with pasta rather than a set of recipes and directions to be followed to the letter, was my daughter Ana's. She was also the driving force behind the project and the talent behind the illustrations.

My part-time vegetarian daughter Bel spent many hours during the summer of her first year in college collecting recipes from napkins and brown paper bags and typing them up on the computer.

My husband Raymond, who likes to eat and whose facial expression after the first bite served as feedback in my test kitchen, dutifully ate many mediocre meals, but also enjoyed all my culinary triumphs.

Lana Merewether, who has a graduate degree in zoology, does my bookkeeping and has also kindly typed draft upon draft of this book. Thank you, Lana. Lucia Greene, who loves the English language as much as chile pasta, had the task of taking my writing—a personal dialect of sorts—and making it intelligible to others. Her suggestions have been valuable to me.

And finally, thanks go to the many friends who have sat at our table and shared with us the experience of celebrating food and being together—and to the customers who have made my flavored pasta shop a success.

Introduction

am not Italian! I was born in the Dominican Republic, a country which shares with Haiti the Caribbean island of Hispaniola and is blessed with coconut groves, banana plantations, and cocoa tree farms where coffee plants grow in the shade of the taller trees.

In the area where I grew up, rice paddies blanketed the valleys, and bean and peanut plots were scattered around. Avocado trees grew everywhere. Oranges, mangos, and giant pineapples were the delights offered as dessert.

The diet was based on root vegetables, rice, beans, and a small amount of meat and cheese. Food was flavored with herbs grown at home or brought in everyday, along with vegetables, by street vendors on burros or bicycles.

And then there was pasta—spaghetti and macaroni to be precise—cooked in many different ways, but somehow never combined with meatballs or meat sauce.

Learning to cook was a traditional part of a girl's upbringing and was more or less an obligatory rite of passage on her way to becoming a wife and mother. Fortunately for me, I liked to cook and was happy to go through the training at my grandmother's side.

There were no cookbooks in my home, nor did I know anyone who had any. Instead there was a continuous exchange of recipes by word of mouth, like an oral history, which ensured each recipe had many variations since every cook added her own embellishments or changed an ingredient or two. All ingredients were fresh and the only thing to come out of a can was tomato paste. Food was always delicious and an important part of life at home.

Both my mother and grandmother were "Sunday cooks" (the cook's day off) but helped out their cooks during the week. They were always learning from each other, swapping cooking tips, and teaching the next generation. Cooking had no mystique; it was nothing to be afraid of, but it helped if you liked to do it or wanted to. In a culture where you didn't get married until you learned to cook, one of my sisters went through training and got married, but has not cooked a thing since!

Many years have passed since I had to prepare a chicken for cooking, and, in those days I had to catch it first! Many trials, many self-taught lessons. The very first cookbook I experimented with was by Julia Child, and many more followed. While in Mexico, I learned Mexican cuisine—no chile con carne there, and a burrito was a small donkey. And, while living in Africa, I learned many oriental, Indian, and Pakistani dishes from the Asian population settled there. It was while living in Nairobi, Kenya that I first made noodles . . . by hand . . . from beginning to end! It was also there that I started putting vegetables in the dough when my children wouldn't eat them otherwise. Today I am putting flavors in noodles and enjoying it. I still feel cooking doesn't have to be complicated; anyone can do it. But more importantly I believe that once you know a general way to cook, you can create your own "cuisine," as pure or adulterated as you please, but uniquely your own.

Of all the regional cuisines I have experienced and experimented with, I have found that Mediterranean in general and Italian in particular lend themselves to creative cooking. My irreverence not being absolute, I think there are some traditional dishes you must not meddle with, mainly out of respect. Your Aunt Mary's lasagna or Uncle Joe's spaghetti sauce may be part of the heritage you need to preserve. But by all means play all you want with Aunt Julie's or Uncle Fred's recipes and you may be on your way to creating your very own cuisine. I do hold respect for regional purist cooks and, indeed, have learned a lot from them, but to put it simply, I like the concept of "doing my own thing" when I cook. That is how some "Indian" spices may end up in an "Italian" dish, or some wonderful curry sauce end up being served on a flavored noodle.

It may be prudent at this point to clarify that although I enjoy creating my own dishes, I don't adhere to the "dump" theory of cooking, where you open a can of this and a can of that and warm it up. Fresh ingredients are a must! If that is too much work, the frozen food sections of the supermarkets have a good selection of frozen fruits and vegetables, but don't compromise when it comes to the quality of your ingredients. (Remember, "garbage in, garbage out"?)

Along with quality ingredients, liking to cook is the most important element in cooking and being able to create your own cuisine. The rest you can learn as you go. You, no doubt, will come up with some dishes you are not proud of, but I can also assure you that your experimentation will create some dishes that may well become "the heritage" you pass on and preserve for the next generation.

About this Book

make pasta for a living! Flavored pastas, that is, ranging from the delicate herbs to the fiery habanero. Born out of necessity, flavored pasta that started as a device to make children eat their vegetables has evolved into a way of bringing flavors to dishes without the need for heavy calorie-laden sauces. But not everyone likes or can eat flavored pasta. Most of the recipes in this book call for flavored pastas, but many have been tested using plain pasta as well. Certainly they won't taste the same—not worse, not better, just different. (Oh, but what an adventure you would miss!)

These recipes are made with pasta, but I would not go as far as calling them Italian. They have a multi-cultural flavor, although it was the creativity of the Italian cooks' insistence on fresh ingredients, and simple culinary traditions that most influenced and inspired this effort.

All the dishes have been developed to be delicious but fairly easy to prepare. The times are gone when spending hours in the kitchen preparing dinner was the thing to do. Today, there are many demands on our time. Easy-to-make is the new approach to nourishment and cooking at home, for family or guests.

The recipes are presented with a "create-your-own-dish" approach. The idea is to learn to prepare good food, not just to follow a recipe. The recipes are presented in a traditional way but at the end of many of them you will find suggestions for substitutions, additions, techniques, and different uses for the same recipe. Follow the recipe as is and you prepare a good dish; follow the suggestions to substitute or add and you will create your own versions, maybe even better than the original. Don't forget that some meat dishes can be transformed into vegetarian ones. The first section deals with different ways to prepare foods for eating as well as a list of basic ingredients to have on hand to make the preparation of pasta dishes an even more expedient process. You will also find a section on making pasta, flavoring pasta, and, most importantly, cooking it right whether store bought, your own, fresh, or dry.

The second section features recipes, grouped according to the main ingredient added to the pasta: vegetables, poultry, seafood, etc. Each chapter has information on handling specific foods, or making the most of the ingredients involved. Or sample polenta and couscous with many of the sauces included in this book. They are fun—and let's face it, sometimes you may want to eat something different from pasta. Just kidding!

Contents

Part One

Chapter 1
Cooking Techniques 8

Chapter 2
Making and Cooking Pasta 12

Chapter 3
Making and Cooking Stuffed Pastas 17

Chapter 4
Planning Meals with Pasta 29

Part Two

Chapter 5
Pesto and Uncooked Vegetable and Herb Sauces 32

Chapter 6
Vegetable and Cheese Pasta Dishes 40

Chapter 7
Cold Pasta Dishes 70

Chapter 8
Vinaigrettes and Dressings 81

Chapter 9
Fish and Seafood Pasta Dishes 88

Chapter 10
Chicken and Pasta Dishes 100

Chapter 11
Pasta Dishes with Red Meat 109

Chapter 12
Polenta, Gnocchi and Couscous 117

Appendix
How to Make Chicken, Beef, Fish and Vegetable Stock 123

Index 126

Order Information 128

Part One

Chapter 1

Cooking Techniques

Usually, there is some preparation involved in making foods ready to eat. The amount of preparation is determined by many different factors: the kinds of food you use (fruit, vegetable, meat, grains, etc.), what you want the end result to be (sautéed, sauce, casserole), what utensils and appliances you have in your kitchen (pots and pans, ovens or grills), and how much time you want to spend preparing and cooking your food (two minutes, one hour, the whole day). The possibilities are as endless as your imagination.

Some foods, of course, require little or no preparation, as they are consumed in their natural state with no cooking involved. With fruit and many vegetables, it is just a matter of washing and/or peeling and cutting—operations that take very little time. Pasta can be prepared in many different ways with many dishes being very easy. The cooking techniques needed are well-known, time-honored methods. Here are some of the more common ones.

1. Boiling

This method of cooking involves immersing the food in boiling water (salted or not) until it acquires the degree of doneness you desire. Many root vegetables are cooked this way, as are many pasta dishes that start by boiling the noodles. Boiling is usually done with high heat at an angry boil (one that cannot be stirred down).

2. Braising

Like boiling, braising involves a liquid such as water, juice, sauce, or broth, which is heated to a slow boil. Herbs and spices are usually added to this liquid, lending their aromas and flavors to the end product. Stews, curries, "guisados," and soups are all examples of braised foods. If the liquid needs to be thickened or reduced, the lid is left off; otherwise it is left on the pot.

Braising is a common method of cooking in places where tender cuts of meat are not readily available or are too expensive.

3. Poaching

Poaching also involves a liquid, flavored or not, but the food cooks at a point below simmering. Simmering is when small bubbles kind of trickle to the surface of the liquid. When done well, foods cooked this way are usually very tender, flavorful, and juicy. Salmon, fowl breasts, and eggs are classic examples of foods cooked this way. Poaching is a preferred way to cook for those watching their diets and especially their fat intake.

To poach a food, select the liquid (water, broth, wine, milk, etc.) and fill a frying pan with 1^1/$_2$ inches of liquid. Heat over medium heat until tiny bubbles form at the bottom of the pan and rise slowly to the surface without breaking it (if the liquid is allowed to boil, meats will get tough). Slowly slide the food into hot liquid, place a lid on it, and cook for the amount of time called for in the recipe. The liquids used for poaching can be used as a base for soups and sauces.

4. Steaming

Steaming is no doubt the best way to cook vegetables since it preserves color and nutrients. When steaming, hot steam does the cooking and the food never comes in contact with the liquid. One important advantage of this method is that vitamins and minerals, some of which can be lost when using other cooking methods, stay in the food when steaming. Also, no fat is needed! There are many gadgets on the market used for this purpose, and meats and vegetables can be cooked at the same time on racks placed over the boiling water and within the steamy vapor.

5. *Blanching*

Blanching is a process by which vegetables are plunged momentarily in boiling water, removed, and quickly placed in cold water to stop the cooking. Blanching loosens the skin of some vegetables and kills the enzymes responsible for ripening. When making pasta and vegetable salads, I prefer to blanch the vegetables, rather than boil them, to keep them crunchy.

6. *Broiling*

Probably the oldest method used to change raw foods into edible ones, broiling can be used with virtually any kind of food. We all recognize the image of our ancestors squatting by the fire and holding a stick laden with what was to become their next meal. This method of cooking involves exposing the food to direct radiant heat from a source a short distance away. It is used for meats, fish, vegetables, and fruit. The barbecue is a good example of broiling and is a favorite in this country for outdoor cooking.

7. *Baking or Roasting*

If a barrier is created (by way of pan, sheet, or oven walls) between the source of heat and the food being cooked, then we are either baking or roasting, and heated air cooks the food. The wonderful array of breads, cakes, pastries, and cookies we can bake stands as a testimony to the usefulness of this age-old method of cooking. When using meats however, we use the term roasting . . . ahh! The Thanksgiving turkey . . . and that savory chicken . . . and the leg of pork or the ham, or just simply "the roast" when we refer to beef . . . A list that can make "meatatarians"[1] jump with joy. Vegetable dishes can also be deliciously prepared with a sauce and baked until done.

[1]A name coined by my daughter, Bel, when she was four. I was explaining the advantages of a vegetarian diet and she decided, then and there, she'd much rather be a meatatarian.

8. Sautéing

In French, the term sauté means "to jump." The food is cooked over a burner (preferably gas) in a very hot pan containing a small amount of oil or seasoned liquid. The pan is rapidly thrust back and forth in such a way as to make the food "jump" and flip so it cooks evenly without burning. (If you have watched cooking shows on television, you have no doubt been impressed by the way the chef sautés the food while amazingly avoiding having it end up on the floor). If sautéing intimidates you, use stir-frying instead.

9. Stir-Frying

As with sautéing, only a small amount of oil is used for stir-frying. Because the foods are cooked at higher temperatures, the solids in butter and margarine will burn and lend a somewhat bitter flavor to foods. When stir-frying, foods are cut into thin, small pieces depending upon the density of the food, so they can all cook evenly. Foods to be cooked using this method should be dry, to avoid splashes and burns, and should be stirred very often to distribute the heat, thus giving the same results as sautéing without the risk of having the food end up all over you. Stir-frying and sautéing are favorite ways to cook pasta dishes throughout this book. They both are very fast and yield delicious results.

10. Frying

I can find only negative things to say about what frying does to foods, arteries, and your health in general. Therefore, I will limit myself to describing what it is.

Frying is a method of cooking foods by immersion in hot fat. Large amounts of fat are usually absorbed by the food, so it is advisable to drain it before eating. Also keep in mind that fat burns are very painful.

Part One

Chapter 2

Making and Cooking Pasta

Many a cook stays away from homemade pasta, thinking that it is an elaborate process that takes much too much time. Actually, making pasta is simple, especially if you have a pasta machine. The dough can be prepared ahead of time and rolled and cut shortly before cooking. Children love helping in this activity, and adults do too. I have had great pasta parties. I prepared different-flavored dough, two or three sauces, made a salad and bread, and the party became alive with conversation, with 'oohs' and 'ahhs' from my guests who enjoyed the meal even more knowing they contributed to it.

Fresh homemade pasta is very different from dry pasta, which has a dense texture and a definite "bite." Freshly-made pasta is softer and more elastic. Semolina, a coarsely-milled flour from winter hard wheat, is ideal for making pasta, but a bit harder to manage if mixing the dough by hand. A half-and-half mixture of semolina and bread flour works well for home use. If semolina is not available, use unbleached, high-gluten bread flour.

Basic Pasta Recipe

Flour and water are all you need to make pasta! Plain pasta that is. But if life is too short for plain noodles, you can flavor your pasta by adding eggs, herbs, vegetables, or spices. But let's start with plain pasta. The process for making pasta is very simple. The proportion of water to flour to produce two servings is as follows:

1/4 cup water
3/4 cup flour

One egg can be substituted for the water, producing a more manageable dough of richer flavor. The dough can be mixed by hand or by using a food processor. If mixing by hand, mound the flour on a flat surface and make a well in the middle. Break the egg in the well, beat it slightly with a fork (or add the water), and start incorporating and mixing flour and egg (or water) to make a dough that is fairly stiff, but that becomes pliable as it is kneaded. If the dough is too stiff, you may want to divide it into three or four portions and knead one at a time until smooth, keeping the others covered to avoid drying.

If mixing in a food processor, place flour in the bowl of the food processor. With the motor running, add the slightly beaten egg (or water) and process for about 60 seconds. Dough should be smooth but not sticky (add more flour if it is sticky). Place dough on a lightly floured counter and knead, incorporating more flour if needed to make the dough a little stiffer.

After the dough is prepared, divide into smaller portions (about the size of an extra-large egg). With your hands, smooth out the portions and place them in a plastic bag or under an inverted bowl. Allow the dough to rest for 20 minutes before rolling by hand or machine.

To roll by hand, place one portion at a time on a slightly floured surface. Stretch with a rolling pin until the dough becomes very thin. Cut with a pastry cutter, using a ruler, into one-quarter inch strips, or roll into a tight tube, cut, and then unroll each section gently and spread out on a towel or hang over a wooden dowel (many children love doing this part) for a few minutes

ravioli cutter

before boiling. These few minutes of rest allow the surface of the noodle to dry slightly, reducing the risk of producing mushy pasta.

If using a hand-cranked machine, take a portion of dough and flatten with a rolling pin until it is thin enough to go through the machine's rollers. Fold and roll at increasingly thinner settings (2 times per setting) until desired thickness. Then pass through cutters and spread on a towel to dry for a few minutes. If the dough tears while going through the machine, it means it is too soft. A bit more flour should be incorporated by sprinkling on both sides of the dough before rolling.

If using an electric pasta maker, follow manufacturer's directions. If the pasta dough is to be used for lasagna, cut into 1^1/2- or 2-inch ribbons. If for cannelloni, cut into 3- or 4-inch squares.

Making Flavored Pastas

Making flavored pastas is also easy to do. However, the basic recipe should be adjusted so that the consistency of the dough is not changed considerably. The nature of the flavoring ingredient will determine the adjustments you need to make. For instance, adding dry herbs and/or black pepper requires no changes, but if you are using a vegetable purée or juice you need to reduce the amount of liquid accordingly. Also keep in mind that some ingredients affect the behavior of the dough. Adding tomato paste, lemon juice, lime juice, or vinegar (all highly acidic) will make pasta more brittle. Here are some ideas. Quantities given are for the Basic Pasta Recipe.

Lemon Pepper: Add 3 tablespoons lime juice, 1 tablespoon lemon zest (yellow part of skin only), and 1 tablespoon black pepper. Increase the amount of flour to 1 cup per egg (instead of ^{3}/4 cup per egg).

Minced Herbs: Use fresh or dry herbs (preferably fresh), finely chopped. No change is required in flour/water or flour/egg ratios.

Basil Garlic: 3 tablespoons fresh basil and 2 cloves of garlic, mashed.

Cilantro Parsley: 3 tablespoons each chopped fresh cilantro and parsley.

Tarragon Lime: 3 tablespoons fresh tarragon, finely chopped, and 1 tablespoon lime zest (green part of skin only).

Chile Flavors: Add 1 or 2 tablespoons of dry red, green, or jalapeño pepper powder to the flour. Because we are adding a dry ingredient to the flour, you may need to use an extra tablespoon of water to reach the right consistency in the dough.

Using Vegetable Purée: A good way to get color in pasta, along with flavor. When using puréed vegetables, increase the amount of flour by 1/2 cup or more, depending upon how runny the purée is. Carrots, beets, spinach, fresh roasted peeled chiles, and bell peppers work very well.

To make a purée, boil peeled vegetables until soft. Purée in a food processor or blender with no water and pass through a strainer. If using · frozen spinach or chiles, process without boiling. Another way to add flavor (and protein) to pasta is by adding a different kind of flour to the basic recipe: whole wheat, cornmeal, blue cornmeal, barley flour, chick-pea flour, lentil flour, etc. Substituting at least 3 tablespoons of semolina with a different flour will change the texture of the dough and make it, in many cases, gummier when cooked. This has to do with the liquid-absorbing properties of the different flours.

How to Cook Perfect Pasta

There is a right way and a wrong way to cook dry pasta. Pasta cooked the right way is firm in texture and the noodles are separate and somewhat chewy (this is known in Italian as "al dente"). Cooking pasta the right way will enhance its flavor and protect its nutritional value. Cooking pasta the wrong way will result in a sticky, gummy, mushy, pasty, or otherwise unappealing noodle. This is the right way:

The key is to use lots of water. Bring a large pot of water (a quart for every 3 ounces of dry pasta) to a rolling boil. The fast boil allows the pasta to circulate for uniform cooking, and the large amount of water keeps it from sticking.

Add the pasta slowly so the water does not stop boiling. If added all at once, the water cools and by the time it boils again, the noodles are overcooked.

Stir often to prevent sticking, and keep the temperature as high as possible without boiling over.

Never cover the pot while it is boiling. If, when adding pasta, the water stops boiling you can hold the lid over the pasta momentarily to return it to a boil, but don't go away if you are at all interested in avoiding an over-spilling mess.

Taste for doneness after 4 minutes. If the center still feels hard and dry, cook longer but test often.

Pasta is done when the hard core in the center is no longer visible. Pasta should be tender but firm or al dente. DO NOT OVERCOOK! Pasta continues to cook even after removed from the burner, so the water should be drained immediately. (Adelina's pastas cook in a shorter time due to the amount of vegetables used to flavor them).

Drain pasta in a colander.

If you are using a sauce, mix your pasta with the sauce and serve at once. If you are using the pasta for a cold dish, after draining, add a bit of olive oil and toss to avoid sticking. Then, spread the pasta on a flat surface to cool. If you are going to use the noodles in a baked dish, undercook them a little.

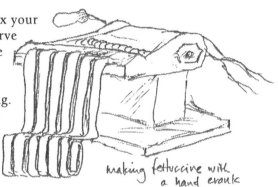

making fettuccine with a hand crank

Do not rinse the pasta unless the recipe says to, or if, by chance, you have overcooked it.

Pasta is best served just after cooking. However, leftovers can be refrigerated and warmed again before eating.

"Cold" pasta dishes should be served at room temperature for peak flavor. If you prepare them ahead of time, refrigerate, but take out one hour before serving. If for some reason you prefer to serve the pasta refrigerator-cold, save some of the dressing and add it just before serving.

If cooking fresh pasta instead of dry, boil for one to two minutes only. Serve at once.

Pasta Has No Patience

Pasta has no patience and once it is cooked it will not wait for you to get the sauce ready. Rather, plan your meal preparation so that the sauce is ready when the pasta is drained. You can then mix and serve right away.

Why does pasta form into a gooey mass of twisted noodles? It cooked too long! If you suspect the pasta is slightly overcooked, place under cold running water after it is drained to stop the cooking. If decisively overcooked, toss away and start over again.

Part One

Chapter 3

Making and Cooking Stuffed Pastas

Now that you feel confident about making fresh pasta, let's get creative and take it a step farther. This section is where the fun really starts, and you may surprise yourself with how many different stuffings you can prepare and how many different shapes you can come up with. The more deliciously unusual the stuffing and shape, the more fun you will have explaining to your guests how you came up with such a dish.

It is useless to try to convince you that making stuffed pastas, whether lasagna, cannelloni, or ravioli is not a bit more involved than buying ready-made from the freezer compartment of your supermarket. However, given the fact that you can make them ahead of time and freeze, and that you know and can control what goes into them, I believe they are well worth the time. Besides, they will be your creation.

When I anticipate entertaining around holidays, I prepare a few recipes of stuffed pasta and store them in the freezer. Then, when the party comes, I bring them out, bake, and serve. They taste as if they were just made.

Planning is important when you want to make stuffed pastas for the freezer. Make it a joint effort with your best friend, your children (it really is fun) or your mate. I usually make stuffed pasta in two sessions. I prepare the stuffing on one day and refrigerate it, which makes it easier to handle. Then the following day I make the pasta, and prepare the morsels. Don't freeze them all! Reward yourself by cooking some for dinner that night.

If you prepare two or three kinds of flavored pastas and stuffings you will have four to nine different possibilities, and that is assuming just one shape. If you introduce another shape, your possibilities grow . . . aren't you clever! (And your show-off potential grows as well).

To make pasta for stuffing, make the dough somewhat softer than for noodles. A softer dough gives a much better seal when making ravioli or tortellini and reduces breakage during cooking.

Basic Recipe for Stuffed Pasta

These are the proportions of ingredients for preparing a dough pliable enough to be used for stuffed pastas:

3/4 cup flour (durum or bread flour)
1 extra-large egg
1 tablespoon water

Of course as is the case when making noodles, you could prepare the pasta with no eggs at all, using only water with the flour:

3/4 cup flour
1/3 cup water

This will give you enough for 9 to 12 raviolis or 6 to 8 cannellonis, depending upon size.

You can also flavor the pasta by using herbs and spices or vegetable purée, but make sure that the flavor you add is very delicate and does not interfere with the flavor of the stuffing.

After the dough is mixed, knead until soft and let it stand for 20 minutes covered with plastic film. Roll out by hand or machine (see instructions for preparing noodles on pages 13–14).

Know Your Stuffed Pastas

Lasagna

Because you need to build layers of pasta and sauce, you need at least a double recipe in order to have enough for a 9x9-inch square pan. Cut the rolled-out dough into 2x8-inch strips (shorter or longer according to the size of the pan you plan to use). Cover the dough strips with a cloth to keep them from drying. When making lasagna with fresh pasta there is no need to boil the strips first, especially if you roll them fairly thin.

Lasagna is better frozen with the sauce already in the baking dish you will use. If you need the baking dish, take frozen contents and wrap well in plastic first and then aluminum foil. Then just place unwrapped block into baking dish when you are ready. When freezing a lasagna for later use, let it come to room temperature before baking until bubbly.

Ravioli

Prepare the stuffing ahead of time. If rolling dough by hand, stretch it until fairly thin. Using a teaspoon, place little mounds of stuffing, all over half of the dough, about 1 inch apart. Brush warm water around the mounds and fold the other half of dough over the stuffing, pressing in between with your fingers or the heel of your hand to seal well. Cut squares with ravioli single cutter or with a cutting wheel. If rolling dough with a machine, place the little mounds over half of the ribbon of dough and moisten in between again to seal. Cut as before. If you get tired of cutting squares, there are other shapes you could explore. Using cookie cutters you can make them round or in any shape. To make tortellini, cut rounds of pasta first. Put a teaspoon of stuffing in the middle, moisten edges and fold in half. Press edges and then, taking pointed edges between thumb and index finger, bring them together and press. Cute!

There are a few gadgets on the market worth investing in, if you like to make stuffed pastas. Ravioli, cannelloni and tortellini makers save time and give a uniform final product. Follow manufacturer's directions.

To cut triangular shapes, cut triangles of dough first, stuff, moisten and seal edges. To make little hats, cut fresh pasta into 3x4-inch rectangles. Place stuffing in the middle, moisten edges and fold the long side of the rectangle in half, then carefully bring the other two sides in in such a way that they all meet at a point on top. Clever! How about using the small thin sheet of pasta as you would to wrap a piece of candy—pressing as you gather the ends to keep filling from coming out.

And you thought I was teasing when I said it was fun!

If you have made more than you can use, place them on a waxed paper-lined cookie sheet in the freezer, then transfer them to freezer bags and squeeze air out before closing. When ready to use, bring out of the freezer and prepare in one of the ways recommended below.

All the little pillows of stuffed pasta, ravioli, tortellini, triangles, rounds, hats, etc., can be served many different ways. Here are some of my favorites: 1) Make a flavorful chicken broth, strain, and use as the liquid to boil them. Serve the broth, and ravioli together as a soup, sprinkled with Parmesan cheese and thinly sliced green onions. 2) Boil the stuffed pasta in salted water, drain, and serve drizzled with olive oil and sprinkled with shredded Parmesan cheese. 3) Place the pasta in a buttered baking dish. Add sliced asparagus and your favorite tomato sauce. Top with shredded mozzarella cheese and bake until golden and bubbly. 4) Stuffed pasta can also be fried, drained on paper towels and served as an appetizer.

Cannelloni

Once the dough is rolled by hand or by machine, cut into 4x4-inch squares. Place a tablespoon of stuffing along one edge of the square and roll, placing seam side down on a plate or baking sheet. Moisten and seal the edge if desired. Cover with cloth and refrigerate until ready to use. Cannelloni can be frozen individually and prepared with the sauce the day you bake them, or prepared with the sauce and frozen for use later.

Green Chile and Herbs Ravioli

Pasta dough made with 2 large eggs, 1³/4 cups flour, ¹/2 cup cilantro and 2 tablespoons water. Prepare according to directions on pages 13–14.

Stuffing

15 ounces ricotta cheese
¹/2 cup green chiles, roasted, cleaned and chopped
¹/4 cup cilantro
1 large egg
¹/2 cup Parmesan cheese, grated
salt and pepper to taste
a pinch of nutmeg

ravioli

Mix all ingredients in a bowl. Refrigerate for 2 hours or overnight. Make the ravioli according to directions on page 19.

Sauce

1 (6-ounce) package Adelina's Green Chile and Romano Pesto Sauce (recipe on page 35)
1 cup cream
salt to taste
sour cream to taste
¹/2 cup Parmesan cheese

If frozen, bring pesto to room temperature. Warm cream and mix with pesto in a saucepan. Heat, but do not boil. Cook ravioli in salted boiling water in a saucepan until tender. Drain and place in serving dish. Pour sour cream over cooked ravioli and sprinkle with the Parmesan cheese. Serve at once. *Serves 4 to 6.*

The following stuffings can be made into any of the shapes discussed earlier. Just make sure the edges are well sealed so the contents don't spill out while cooking. Serve as soon as they are ready with a tasty sauce.

Green Chile Stuffing for Cannelloni

20 ounces ricotta cheese
4 to 6 canned or frozen green chiles, diced
1 egg
2 tablespoons cilantro
1 teaspoon each salt and pepper
1 tablespoon olive oil
Porcini Tomato Sauce (page 55)

Mix first 7 ingredients in a bowl. Use for stuffing cannelloni. Place in buttered dish and cover with Porcini Tomato Sauce. Bake for 20 to 25 minutes. Serve at once. *Makes 18 cannelloni.*

Ricotta, Green Chile and Fresh Herb Stuffing

1 large onion, finely chopped
6 tablespoons olive oil
1 1/2 cups ricotta cheese
1/2 tablespoon dry oregano
4 large green chiles, roasted, peeled and finely chopped
1/4 cup fresh cilantro
salt and pepper to taste
1 egg

Over medium heat, sauté the onion in olive oil in a sauté pan until soft and golden brown. Set aside; let cool to room temperature. When cooled, place in a bowl and add ricotta cheese, oregano, chiles and fresh cilantro. Season with salt and pepper to taste. In a bowl, beat the egg slightly, add to ricotta/chile and mix. Chill, covered, for 2 hours or overnight.

To shape your stuffed pasta, follow directions on page 19. Serve boiled shapes drained and drizzled with olive oil and sprinkled with Parmesan cheese if desired. *Makes 18 small shapes.*

Salmon and Leeks Cannelloni

This makes a good stuffing for cannelloni, but can be made into other shapes as well.

Pasta dough made with 2 large eggs, 1³/4 cups flour and ¹/2 cup chopped parsley, following the directions on pages 13–14, 20.

Stuffing

1 pound cooked salmon (poached or baked works best), flaked
¹/3 cup chives, finely chopped
1 teaspoon garlic, minced
¹/2 cup chopped leeks, sautéed in olive oil
1 cup cooked vegetables (zucchini, broccoli, bell peppers, etc.) cut into very fine strips
1 teaspoon ground white pepper
1 tablespoon chopped fresh dill
salt (if desired)

Mix all ingredients in a bowl and refrigerate for 3 hours or overnight. Use to stuff cannelloni.

Dill Yogurt and Mushroom Sauce

1 onion, chopped
¹/2 pound mushrooms, sliced
¹/4 cup olive oil
¹/2 cup dry white wine
¹/4 cup sour cream
¹/2 cup yogurt
1 teaspoon dill weed, finely chopped
¹/4 teaspoon cayenne pepper powder
salt and pepper

Sauté onion and mushrooms in oil in sauté pan. Add wine and cook for approximately 5 minutes to reduce by half. Combine all other ingredients, add to sauté pan and warm thoroughly (don't allow to boil). Spoon over boiled cannelloni or your chosen shape. Makes 18 cannelloni or 25 ravioli. *Serves 4 to 6.*

Scallops and Spinach Cannelloni

Stuffing

1 tablespoon olive oil
1 onion, finely chopped
1 (16-ounce) package frozen spinach leaves, chopped
1 pound bay scallops, chopped
salt and pepper to taste
1 tablespoon fresh basil, chopped
1 tablespoon lime juice
3/4 cup ricotta cheese

In a sauté pan heat olive oil. Add onion, spinach and scallops and sauté for five minutes. (The mixture should be dry). Sprinkle with salt and pepper to taste. Remove from heat. When cool, add the rest of the ingredients. Adjust salt and pepper. Use to stuff cannelloni or ravioli. Pages 13–14, 19–20 contain instructions.

Sauce

1/2 cup water
1/2 cup white wine
2 tablespoons green onions, chopped
1 tablespoon parsley
1/8 tablespoon cayenne pepper powder
1/8 teaspoon salt (if desired)
1/2 cup Parmesan cheese
1/2 cup cream

Mix all ingredients except cream in a saucepan and cook for 10 to 15 minutes or until reduced by 1/3. Add cream and simmer until thick. Place cannelloni or ravioli in a buttered baking dish. Spoon the sauce over stuffed pasta and bake for 20 to 25 minutes. Serve at once. *Serves 4 to 6.*

limes

Meat Stuffing

2 cups leftover chopped cooked meat (chicken, pork, roast beef)
3/4 pound mushrooms, chopped
4 cloves of garlic
1 teaspoon thyme leaves
1 egg
2 cups provolone cheese, shredded
1/2 cup parsley
1 teaspoon habanero hot sauce
salt and pepper to taste

Combine all ingredients in a bowl. Place in food processor 1/2 at a time and, using the "pulse" button, process 6 or 7 times. Return to the bowl and refrigerate until ready to use.

 ဢ *With the exception of Thanksgiving and Christmas, it is not very often that I have 2 cups of meat left over. One could very well cook some meat just for the purpose of making stuffed pastas. A well-flavored Italian sausage does very well.*

Crab Meat and Shrimp Stuffing

1/2 pound shrimp, steamed for 2 minutes and peeled
1/2 pound crab meat, fresh or frozen
4 green onions
3/4 cup ricotta cheese
2 tablespoons chopped fresh tarragon leaves
2 tablespoons whipping cream
1 tablespoon melted butter
salt and pepper to taste

Place all ingredients in the bowl of a food processor. Process until well blended.

Ham and Tomato Basil Lasagna

Pasta dough made with 2 large eggs, 1¾ cups flour, and one 16-ounce package frozen spinach. Add more flour if needed to make a stiff dough. Roll thin and cut into eight 2x12-inch strips and eight 2x9-inch strips. See page 18.

1 cup grated Parmesan cheese
1 cup toasted bread crumbs
10 ounces mozzarella cheese
2 teaspoons chopped garlic
4 pounds ripe tomatoes,
    peeled, cut into strips
1 cup chopped basil
    leaves
2/3 cup (more or less) olive
    oil
8 ounces prosciutto ham, thinly sliced and
    chopped
salt and freshly ground pepper
    to taste

tomato

Preheat the oven to 375 degrees.

Reserve 1/3 cup of the Parmesan cheese and 1/3 cup of the bread crumbs for topping.

Julienne the mozzarella cheese. Combine with garlic, tomatoes, basil, 1/3 cup of the olive oil, remaining 2/3 cup of the Parmesan cheese, prosciutto salt and pepper in a bowl.

Arrange 4 long strips of pasta on bottom of buttered 9x12-inch pan. Add layers of filling and bread crumbs. Layer short strips of pasta in the opposite direction and repeat until everything is used up. Sprinkle the top with the reserved Parmesan cheese and bread crumbs. Bake for 20 to 25 minutes or until golden. *Serves 4 to 6.*

Lasagna New Mexico

Chopped hot green chiles take this dish from "Mamma Mia" to "Olé!"

To make the noodles, make a double recipe of the dough as it appears on page 18. Add a tablespoon of freshly ground colored peppercorns to the flour before adding the liquid. After noodles are cut, cover with a cloth to keep from drying.

Meat Sauce

1/4 cup dried porcini mushrooms
2 tablespoons olive oil
1 large onion, finely chopped
3 cloves of garlic, crushed
1 large rib of celery, thinly sliced
1 large green bell pepper, diced
1 cup chopped fresh mushrooms
8 hot green chiles, roasted, peeled, chopped
1 1/2 pounds extra-lean ground beef
1/2 pound extra-lean ground pork
1 (12-ounce) can tomato paste
2 cups beef broth
1/2 cup dry white wine
2 tablespoons parsley
salt and pepper

White Sauce

1/4 cup butter
1/4 cup olive oil
1 cup flour
1 quart skim milk
1 teaspoon salt
pepper to taste
a pinch of nutmeg
4 ounces shaved Parmesan cheese (use a vegetable peeler on a chunk of fresh Parmesan cheese)
4 ounces shredded mozzarella cheese

dried porcini mushrooms

Place dried mushrooms in a bowl, cover them with hot water and soak for 30 minutes. Drain, strain the liquid and save. Finely chop the drained mushrooms.

In a large pot, heat the olive oil and sauté the onion and garlic for 5 minutes over medium heat, stirring often.

Add celery, green pepper, fresh mushrooms and chiles and cook 3 minutes longer. Remove to a dish and keep warm.

Using the same pot (no need to rinse) brown the meats well for about 15 minutes, breaking big lumps as they form. Add tomato paste, chopped dried mushrooms, broth, wine and the water reserved from soaking the mushrooms. Bring to a boil and simmer for 45 minutes.

Add the sautéed vegetables and chopped parsley and cook for another 15 to 20 minutes. Taste and add salt and pepper as desired. Remove from heat.

To make the white sauce, melt the butter and mix with oil in a saucepan. Stir in 1 cup flour until all is absorbed by the butter and oil mixture. Remove from heat and start adding the milk slowly while stirring constantly until the milk is used up. Make sure there are no lumps.

Return to the heat and cook over low heat until thick and smooth, stirring constantly. Add salt, pepper and nutmeg.

To assemble, butter a 9x13-inch baking dish. Place 1/2 cup of meat sauce in the bottom. Cover with noodles. Layer meat sauce, white sauce, Parmesan cheese and noodles until all is used up.*

Sprinkle mozzarella cheese all over before baking in a 350-degree oven for 40 minutes.

*At this point it can be frozen. Bring to room temperature before adding mozzarella and baking.

Spinach and Crab Meat Cannelloni

Stuffing
12 cannelloni tubes or 4x4-inch squares of fresh dough
1 tablespoon olive oil
2 cloves of garlic, crushed
1 medium onion, chopped
3 green onions, chopped
10 ounces frozen chopped spinach
2 tablespoons fresh basil, cut into strips
2 tablespoons lime juice
8 ounces crab meat, cleaned, flaked
3/4 cup ricotta cheese
salt and pepper to taste

garlic

Sauce
1/2 cup skim milk
1/2 cup dry white wine or flavored broth
3 ounces cream cheese, diced
1 tablespoon chopped fresh basil
salt and freshly ground pepper to taste
2 tablespoons sliced green onions
1/2 cup shredded mozzarella cheese

If using commercial cannelloni tubes, prepare by the package instructions. If using fresh dough, there is no need to boil them first.

In a skillet, heat the olive oil and sauté garlic and onion for 10 minutes or until onion becomes golden. Stir in green onions, spinach, basil and 1 tablespoon of the lime juice; cook for 2 minutes and remove from heat.

Add crab meat, ricotta cheese and the rest of the lime juice, salt and pepper. While mixture cools, prepare the sauce. In a small saucepan, mix milk and wine and heat over low heat. Add cream cheese and stir until melted. Add basil, salt, pepper and green onions and cook until reduced by 1/4 or for approximately 7 minutes.

Stuff cannelloni with the crab mixture and place in buttered dish. Drizzle with sauce and bake, covered, for 20 minutes. Uncover, sprinkle with mozzarella and bake for 15 minutes to brown slightly. *Serves 4 to 6.*

Part One

Chapter 4

Planning Meals with Pasta

If I have failed to convince you that making pasta can be easy and a lot of fun, there are still innumerable ways to enjoy pasta, plain or flavored. I believe in pasta. After more than 20 years of cooking, experimenting with colors, textures, and flavors and learning to cook in different styles, East and West, I have concluded that there are few foods as perfect as pasta.

With the hundreds of shapes and many flavors available in the market today, versatility is one of its main attributes. It can be served hot, at room temperature, or cold; for lunch or dinner (breakfast or dessert, too); as a main dish, salad or soup; or to accompany meat, poultry, or seafood. It can be boiled, baked, stuffed, smothered, tossed, and even fried.

The wonders of pasta go beyond its versatility and taste. In addition to being delicious, pastas especially seasoned (not just colored) pastas are amazingly easy to prepare. Also, as economic demands and cultural changes bring more mothers into the work force, the time available for meal preparation is rapidly shrinking and eating out is not always an option. Pasta is an easy-to-digest, appealing food that makes sense for people of all ages. It is low in fat, sodium, cholesterol, and calories and is the perfect accompaniment for vegetables, legumes, meats, and seafood.

Whether cooking for one or feeding the soccer team, pasta is a valuable ally. Cooked in single portions or in large amounts for family meals or entertaining, it will always make a tasty and nutritious meal.

Nutritionally, pasta is a must. It is a nutrition-dense carbohydrate, providing more important nutrients than calories per serving. Pasta, a complex carbohydrate, must be broken into simpler forms, thus "supplying the brain and muscles a slower, constant source of energy,"[2] an advantage for athletes who "carbo-load" before a competition to increase glycogen reserves that are then released slowly during prolonged physical exertion.

[2]Facts on Pasta. Nutritional Pasta Association

Pasta can be a one-dish meal, especially if you keep a few essentials on hand:

Olive Oil: A good, dark, extra-virgin, cold-press olive oil is essential for pasta salads, for cooking many pasta sauces, or for drizzling over just-cooked pasta.

Parmesan Cheese: A chunk of it to grate as you need it or a good quality grated cheese with no additives or preservatives (anti-oxidants or anti-caking agents). Use for making sauces or for sprinkling over pasta dishes. Chunk Parmesan or Romano cheese keeps well in the refrigerator if placed in tightly closed jar.

Feta Cheese: Very good for making sauces, or just crumbled and served over hot or cold pasta. If the cheese is too salty, place it in a container and cover it with tap water. Change water often to reduce salinity and keep fresh.

Ricotta Cheese: Excellent choice for stuffings for ravioli or cannelloni or in making lasagna. Also used in preparing some dessert dishes.

Olives: Italian, Greek, American, green or ripe, plain or stuffed, olives add flavor to cold or hot dishes. If using in a sauce, add just before it finishes cooking. Texture and flavor of olives change dramatically when cooked for long periods of time.

Capers: Good in the preparation of many salads and hot dishes. If you are concerned about sodium, limit their use, or blanch them before using. They are very flavorful.

Garlic: Fresh whenever possible, in a jar if you must. Garlic is a wonderful beginning for many a pasta dish.

Peppercorns: Black, white, green, or red. Always freshly ground.

Dried Tomatoes: Dice or cut into julienne strips. They can be used as such or steeped in olive oil for sauces or tossing with finished dish.

Green Chiles: From your freezer. This addition makes sense to pasta eaters in the U.S. Southwest. For sauces or stuffings or toppings.

Herbs: Basil, rosemary, parsley, and oregano are basic herbs for flavoring pasta and many other dishes. They add the most flavor when fresh, but can be used dry too. As dry herbs age, they lose the essential oils that flavor them. Fresh herbs are available all year round in the fresh-produce section of your supermarkets. They also grow well in pots on a sunny windowsill or in your garden. If you grow more than you can use during the summer, here is a way to keep a bit of summer flavor during the winter months. Rinse the herb leaves and dry very gently to avoid bruising. Place in a sterilized jar. Cover with olive oil and lid. Place in refrigerator until ready to use. The leaves will darken but they still taste great in sauces and dressings. Another method that works well, especially with basil, is to place the rinsed, dried leaves in the food processor, adding 1/4 cup olive oil per 1 cup of packed leaves. Process to make a paste and freeze in small ice cube trays. When frozen, remove from trays to a freezer container, place in freezer, and use 1 "basil ice cube" as you need it in your recipes. If you're endowed with patience, there is yet a better way. Once the leaves are rinsed and patted dry, carefully place one at a time, single-layered, on a baking sheet. Place in freezer and, once frozen, remove and place into sealable plastic bags. Using this last method keeps the color as well. Your patience will be rewarded.

Pine Nuts: A perfect sprinkle for all kinds of pasta dishes. A must in the preparation of pesto sauces.

Frozen Vegetables and Legumes: Peas, black-eyed peas, garbanzos, spinach, lima beans, asparagus. All add color, texture, vitamins, and protein.

Fresh Vegetables: Bell peppers, green onions, eggplant, broccoli, mushrooms, and many other vegetables can be easily incorporated into pasta dishes of all kinds.

Canned Foods: Italian Roma tomatoes, anchovies, mussels, oysters, and dried smoked salmon.

Vinegar: Wine vinegar or balsamic vinegar for pasta salads.

Broth: Homemade is preferable (see appendix for recipes) or use flavored granules to prepare. There are many products on the market for making meat or vegetable broths. Avoid, if you can, any with monosodium glutamate. It does nasty things to your taste buds.

Part Two

Chapter 5

Pesto and Uncooked Vegetable and Herb Sauces

Pesto is an uncooked sauce made with fresh herbs, Parmesan cheese, olive oil, and nuts. The traditional pesto (originated in Genoa, Italy) is made with fresh basil leaves and pine nuts mixed with the other ingredients and crushed together with a mortar and pestle. Originally developed as a pasta sauce, pesto has found many uses in modern cooking: as a topping for baked potatoes, a spread for bread, a stuffing for meats and vegetables, or just added to soups before serving. Mixed with vinegar and oil it also makes an excellent dressing for pasta, beans, or green salads.

mushroom, oil & spices

Basil Pesto

One of the real pleasures of summer!

**2 cups fresh basil (lightly rinse leaves so as not to rub off the natural oils
on the leaves that contribute to its flavor and wonderful smell)**
1/3 cup olive oil
1/2 cup grated Parmesan cheese
2 large cloves of garlic, crushed
1/2 teaspoon salt
1/2 teaspoon freshly ground pepper
3 tablespoons pine nuts

Place clean basil leaves in a food processor container and finely chop. Add
oil, Parmesan cheese, garlic, salt and pepper. Process until smooth. Add
the pine nuts and turn on/off a couple of times. Makes approximately 1
cup. *Serves 6 to 8.*

Variations

*If basil is not your favorite herb, try substituting all or part of the basil with
fresh spinach leaves, parsley, or cilantro.*

A New Mexican touch?

*Drop a freshly roasted and seeded green chile (or 2 or 3 . . .) into the
mixture.*

Like creamed pesto?

Add 3 tablespoons heavy cream.

Want to serve it during winter?

*Make it during the summer and freeze in an ice
cube tray. When frozen, remove little pesto blocks
from tray and place in proper freezer container. Then
take out 1 or 2 blocks as needed.*

mushrooms

Parsley Anchovy Pesto

6 ounces anchovy fillets
4 cloves of garlic
2 cups parsley
1 teaspoon fresh thyme
3/4 cup olive oil
1/2 cup bread crumbs
1/4 cup grated Romano cheese
1/2 cup pecans

Process all ingredients in a food processor.

Serve over hot cooked pasta or on rounds of toasted French bread. Makes approximately 1 1/2 cups. Use 2 tablespoons for each serving of pasta. Freeze leftover pesto. *Serves 8 to 10.*

Black Olives and Red Chile Pesto

1 cup fresh red chiles, roasted
1/2 cup piñon nuts
1 tablespoon vegetable or olive oil
2 cups pitted black olives
3 cloves of garlic
1 bunch parsley
1 cup olive oil
1 cup grated Parmesan cheese
salt and pepper to taste

In a food processor, finely chop the red chiles and place in a bowl with the piñon nuts. Pour 1 tablespoon of oil over top.

Add all other ingredients to the food processor container and process until smooth. Add this to the red chiles and the piñon nuts and mix together. Serve over hot cooked pasta. Use 2 tablespoons pesto per serving of pasta. Leftovers can be frozen for later use.

ఴ *Try with any of Adelina's pastas or, if you must, over plain noodles.*

Pistachio Basil Pesto

Toasting the pistachios and the pine nuts for 10 minutes in a 350-degree oven will bring out the flavor.

1 cup pistachio meats, toasted
1 cup pine nuts, toasted
1 tablespoon garlic, crushed
1 cup grated Parmesan cheese
3 cups fresh basil (lightly rinse leaves so as not to rub off the natural oils on the leaves that contribute to its flavor and wonderful smell)
2 cups olive oil
1/2 teaspoon salt (if desired)

In a food processor bowl, place 1/2 cup of the pistachios, 1/2 cup of the pine nuts, garlic, Parmesan cheese and basil. Process to a thick paste. Slowly pour in the oil, processing until smooth. Add remainder of nuts and pulse processor to chop. Add salt if needed. Toss with hot cooked pasta (add 2 or 3 tablespoons per serving). Freeze remaining pesto in ice cube tray. When frozen, transfer to airtight container and keep frozen. Bring to room temperature before serving.

Green Chile and Romano Pesto Sauce

2 cups fresh green chiles, roasted and cleaned, or canned chiles
1 cup pecans
1 cup grated Romano cheese
1/2 cup cilantro
4 cloves of garlic
1 cup olive oil
salt and freshly ground pepper

Coarsely chop green chiles and pecans. Mix remaining ingredients except oil in a food processor, pulsing until chopped. Then using continuous speed, process while pouring oil over the top. Add salt and pepper. Use immediately over hot cooked pasta, 2 tablespoons per serving. Refrigerate for up to 6 hours. Freeze for longer storage.
Serves 6 to 8.

Peppers Pesto

2 cups roasted red or green bell peppers
1 cup roasted red or green chiles
1 cup olive oil
1¹/₂ cups grated Parmesan cheese
1¹/₂ cups chopped pecans
6 cloves of garlic, chopped
1 bunch parsley
salt and pepper

Choose either all red or all green bell peppers and chiles (the mixture of red and green when ground together acquires an unappetizing color).* Chop coarsely and place in a food processor container. Add the remaining ingredients and process until mixed well. Serve over hot cooked pasta, 2 or 3 tablespoons per serving. *Makes approximately 4 cups.*

On the other hand, if they are sliced very thinly and mixed by hand rather than in the food processor, the mixture of colors works well.

Dried Tomato Pesto

2 cups boiling water
2 cups coarsely chopped dried tomatoes
4 cloves of garlic, crushed
1 cup grated Parmesan cheese
1 cup olive oil
1/2 cup basil leaves, chopped
3/4 cup pine nuts
salt and freshly ground peppercorns

Pour 2 cups boiling water over chopped dried tomatoes. Soak for 5 minutes and drain, reserving liquid. Place tomatoes in food processor. Add garlic and Parmesan cheese and process with on/off action until mixed. Leave the power on and slowly pour in the oil, processing until smooth.* Add remaining ingredients. Process again, using on/off action to coarsely chop and mix. If the mixture is too solid, add 1 or 2 tablespoons of the tomato soaking liquid. *Makes 4 cups, enough for 8 to 10 servings.*

If you like more texture, process using the on/off action until mixed.

Pesto and Poultry in Cold Pasta Dishes

1 pound Green Chile Pasta, cooked, drained, and cooled to room
  temperature
1 tablespoon olive oil
2 cups frozen peas
2 cups leftover chicken, boned and diced
1 cup of your favorite pesto
1/4 cup grated Parmesan cheese

Toss pasta with olive oil in a large bowl.

Place peas in a colander and hold under running hot water until thawed.
Add peas and diced chicken to pasta. Toss with pesto and sprinkle with
Parmesan cheese. Serve at room temperature. *Serves 6 to 8.*

cs *This dish makes a great dinner for family and friends when served with a
tossed green salad, a loaf of bread, and your favorite wine. It is my number
one choice for feeding a crowd at a church or sports function or any other
occasion where the number of people is a consideration. You can double,
triple, etc. the recipe. It can be prepared ahead of time, and if you don't
have leftover chicken, buy a rotisserie bird, remove the skin, fat and bones,
and you are ready to go.*

cs *If the pasta is cooked right (firm to the bite), leftovers are good enough for
a second set of friends the next day.*

green chile

Pesto-Stuffed Mushrooms

16 large fresh mushroom caps
salt to taste
1 tablespoon olive oil
1 cup Basil Pesto (page 33)
1/4 cup bread crumbs
1/4 cup finely chopped parsley

Clean mushroom caps and drop in salted boiling water in saucepan for just 2 minutes. Drain. Brush with olive oil. Fill each cap with about 1 tablespoon of the pesto and place in buttered dish. Sprinkle with a mixture of bread crumbs, chopped parsley and any remaining olive oil. Bake in a preheated 375-degree oven for 15 minutes or until soft. *Serves 4 to 6.*

Black Pepper Rigatoni and Pesto

4 ounces pesto, your own or bought
2 tablespoons lime juice
2 tablespoons mild olive oil
1 cup frozen peas
1/4 cup pine nuts, toasted
10 ounces Black Pepper Rigatoni
1/4 cup coarsely grated Parmesan cheese

In a small bowl, place the pesto, lime juice and oil. Mix well. Add peas and pine nuts. Set aside. Cook the rigatoni al dente. Drain and rinse with cold water to stop the cooking. Shake all water out. Mix pesto and rigatoni and sprinkle with Parmesan cheese. *Serves 4 to 6.*

New Mexican rigatoni

Other Uses for Pesto

- ❀ Toss with hot cooked pastas

- ❀ Spoon into soups

- ❀ Spread on toasted French bread

- ❀ Mix with cream cheese for spread

- ❀ Mix with boiled potatoes for side dish

- ❀ Serve over baked potatoes

- ❀ **As a spread:** Mix $1/2$ cup pesto and 8 ounces cream cheese in food processor until well blended. Pour into a bowl and refrigerate until ready to use. Serve with crackers.

- ❀ **As a dip:** Mix $1/2$ cup pesto, 6 ounces cream cheese and $1/2$ cup sour cream in food processor. Serve in a bowl surrounded with fresh vegetables.

- ❀ **As a topping for baked potatoes:** Split 2 large potatoes, baked or cooked in a microwave oven, and top with $1/2$ cup pesto.

- ❀ **Pesto on poultry:** Flatten 2 halved skinned chicken breasts (4 pieces). Rinse chicken and pat dry with paper towels. Sprinkle with pepper and a bit of salt. Place chicken in a buttered dish. Spoon $1/4$ cup pesto over each chicken breast. Bake, covered, in a preheated 350-degree oven for 15 minutes. Uncover and bake for another 7 to 10 minutes.

- ❀ **To serve with French bread as an appetizer:** Cut a loaf of French bread into $1/2$-inch thick rounds and place on baking sheet. Brush with olive oil and toast the bread. Serve pesto in a bowl surrounded by toasted bread rounds.

Part Two

Chapter 6

Vegetable and Cheese Pasta Dishes

The variety of common and exotic vegetables found in the stores throughout the year offers the cook of today many choices for interesting and tasty vegetable and pasta combinations for family meals or entertainment.

When buying vegetables, remember that they deteriorate very quickly, so buy what you can use in 2 or 3 days (a week at the most). Refrigerate until ready to use. Wash vegetables well before using to rid them of any pesticide residue (unless, of course, you buy organic).

For convenience, frozen vegetables are hard to match. They are usually processed soon after harvesting and are cleaned and ready to use. Because they are blanched before packaging, most require minimum cooking time. Frozen vegetables retain more nutrients than those packaged in a can.

In this section we also include legumes, which can supply, along with vitamins and minerals, a complete protein meal when combined in the right proportion with pasta (a fact well appreciated by vegetarians all over the world).

asparagus

Red Chile Pasta with Vegetables

3 tablespoons pine nuts
5 tablespoons olive oil
4 very young (3/4-inch diameter) zucchini, sliced
4 very small yellow squash, sliced
6 green onions (whites only), thinly sliced
1 teaspoon crushed garlic
1 (4-ounce) can each bamboo shoots and water chestnuts, rinsed
salt and pepper to taste
10 ounces Red Chile Pasta, cooked, drained
1/4 pound feta cheese, diced

In a sauté pan over medium heat, brown pine nuts in 1 tablespoon of the oil until golden brown. Remove from pan. Add remaining oil and when hot, sauté zucchini, squash, green onions, garlic, bamboo shoots and water chestnuts for 2 to 3 minutes. Add salt and pepper to taste. Toss with cooked hot pasta and sprinkle with cheese. *Serves 6.*

Red Chile Pasta and Cheese

1/4 cup butter or margarine
2 tablespoons olive oil
1/4 cup flour
2 cups milk
1 teaspoon red chile flakes
freshly ground pepper
a pinch of cumin
10 ounces Red Chile Pasta
3 cups shredded Monterey Jack cheese

Preheat oven to 350 degrees. Melt butter or margarine in a saucepan; mix in the olive oil. Add flour and cook over medium heat for 3 to 4 minutes, stirring constantly. Remove from heat and stir in milk slowly. Return to heat. Bring to a boil and cook until thick and shiny, stirring constantly. Add red chile flakes, freshly ground pepper and cumin. Cook pasta in a large pot until al dente. Drain and mix with white sauce and shredded cheese. Bake in buttered baking dish for 20 to 25 minutes or until bubbly. *Serves 6.*

Jalapeño Fettuccine with Roasted Garlic

6 heads of garlic
1/4 cup extra-virgin olive oil
1/4 cup dry tomato flakes
salt and pepper
1 tablespoon finely chopped parsley
1 pound Jalapeño Fettuccine
2 ounces Parmesan cheese, shaved into curls with a potato peeler

Cut 3/4 inch from tops of garlic*. Wrap each in foil and place on a fireproof dish in a preheated 350-degree oven. Bake for 45 minutes or until garlic feels soft when pressure is applied.

Allow the garlic to cool enough to be handled. Then unwrap and squeeze the cloves out of their skins into a medium bowl. Add the olive oil, dry tomato flakes, salt, pepper and parsley. Mash all together and set aside.

In a large pot of boiling salted water, cook the fettuccine until al dente. Drain and place in a serving bowl. Add the garlic sauce and toss gently. Scatter the Parmesan curls over it. Serve at once. *Serves 6 to 8.*

If garlic is not your bulb, try small roasted onions.

Green Chile Pasta with Porcini Sauce

1/3 ounce dry porcini mushrooms, soaked in hot water for 30 minutes, rinsed, and strained through coffee filter (reserve liquid)
2 tablespoons olive oil
1 large onion, thinly sliced top to bottom
2 large cloves of garlic, crushed
2 green chiles, roasted, cleaned, diced
2 bell peppers, roasted, cleaned, diced
salt and freshly ground pepper to taste
1/2 teaspoon oregano
1/2 cup cream
1 pound Green Chile Pasta
1/4 cup parsley

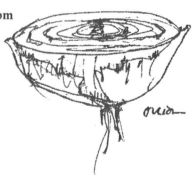

onion

Chop mushrooms well.

In skillet, heat 2 tablespoons oil over medium heat and sauté onion, garlic and chopped mushrooms for about 5 minutes. Add chiles, bell peppers, salt, pepper and oregano and cook for another 3 minutes. Add cream and 1/2 cup liquid from mushrooms and cook to reduce liquids by 1/2 (about 5 minutes).

Meanwhile, bring a large pot of water to a boil. Cook pasta until al dente and drain. Toss pasta with sauce and serve sprinkled with parsley. *Serves 4 to 6.*

cs *Adding 1/4 pound prosciutto ham, cut in ribbons, makes this dish quite wonderful. Add it at the same time you add the chiles.*

Herb-Speckled Pasta with Garlic and Fresh Basil

If you like garlic, this dish will please your palate. Other flavors of pasta will go well with the garlic, too.

3 tablespoons olive oil
10 large cloves of garlic, sliced
1 pound Herb-Speckled Linguine
2 tablespoons unsalted butter
salt and pepper (if desired)
1 cup grated Parmesan cheese
1/2 cup fresh basil, sliced

Bring a large pot of salted water to a boil.

Using a large skillet, heat the olive oil over medium heat. Add the garlic and lower the heat to the lowest setting. Cook, covered, for 6 minutes. Uncover and continue to cook over lowest heat for about 10 minutes. (The garlic should look very pale yellow. If garlic turns gold or brown it will also turn bitter.) When garlic is almost done, boil the pasta in a large pot until tender but still firm to the tooth. Drain. Immediately add to garlic, along with the butter. Toss well. Sprinkle with Parmesan cheese and basil. Serve at once. *Serves 6 to 8.*

cs *A teaspoon of a good-quality balsamic vinegar on each serving adds a wonderful quality to this dish.*

Cream and Wine Primavera

4 green onions, finely chopped
1 teaspoon crushed garlic
1/4 cup unsalted butter
2 cups seasonal vegetables (choose from carrots, garden peas, zucchini,
    mushrooms, asparagus, bell peppers and eggplant)
1 1/4 cups dry white wine
1 1/2 cups whipping cream
10 ounces Green or Red Chile Pasta
1/2 cup grated Parmesan cheese
1/4 cup chopped parsley
salt and pepper

In a large skillet, sauté green onions and garlic in butter over medium
heat for 2 minutes. Raise heat, add vegetables and sauté for 3 minutes.
Remove and keep warm. Add wine to hot skillet and boil for 6 minutes or
until reduced by 1/2. Add the cream and cook for 8 to 10 minutes or until
sauce is thickened. Stir in the vegetables and heat through. Boil the pasta
until al dente. Drain. Add Parmesan cheese, parsley, salt and pepper to
vegetable mixture. Serve over hot pasta. *Serves 4.*

Olive Oil Primavera

4 cloves of garlic, sliced
1/4 cup olive oil
chopped onion to taste
2 cups seasonal vegetables (carrots, garden peas, zucchini, yellow squash,
    mushrooms, asparagus, bell peppers or eggplant)
10 ounces Herb-Speckled Pasta
2 tablespoons parsley
salt and pepper
2 tablespoons grated Romano cheese
1/2 cup crumbled feta cheese

Sauté garlic in olive oil in sauté pan until golden. Discard garlic. Raise the
heat, stir-fry onion and vegetables until tender-crisp. Boil the pasta in a
large pot until al dente. Drain. Add parsley, salt and pepper and serve over
hot pasta. Sprinkle Romano and feta cheese over top. *Serves 4.*

Very Low-Calorie Tomato Basil Primavera

1 small onion, finely chopped
1 teaspoon crushed garlic
1 tablespoon extra-virgin olive oil
1 (15-ounce) can Italian plum tomatoes
1 tablespoon tomato paste
1/2 teaspoon dry oregano
1 tablespoon chopped fresh basil (or 1/2 teaspoon dried)
salt and pepper to taste
2 cups seasonal vegetables (carrots, garden peas, zucchini, yellow squash,
    mushrooms, asparagus, bell peppers or eggplant)
10 ounces Tomato Basil Garlic Pasta
Parmesan cheese to taste

In a skillet over medium heat, sauté onion and garlic in the olive oil for 3
minutes. Add the tomatoes and tomato paste; cook for 2 minutes. Then
add herbs, spices and 2 cups fresh vegetables. Simmer until thick. Boil the
pasta in a large pot until tender but still firm to the tooth. Drain. Spoon
sauce over hot cooked pasta and sprinkle with Parmesan cheese. *Serves 4.*

Pasta Putanesca

1/4 cup olive oil
1 large onion, chopped
4 cloves of garlic, chopped
1/2 pound bacon, crisp-fried, drained, crumbled
1 (2-pound) can Italian plum tomatoes, drained, chopped
1 teaspoon oregano
1/8 teaspoon hot pepper flakes
1/2 cup black olives
1/2 cup parsley, chopped
10 ounces Tomato Basil Garlic Pasta

Heat olive oil in a large skillet over moderate heat. Sauté onion and garlic
until tender. Add bacon crumbs and cook for 1 minute. Add next 5
ingredients and cook until thickened to your liking. Boil pasta in a large
pot until tender but still firm to the tooth. Drain and serve with sauce. If
desired, sprinkle with Parmesan cheese. *Serves 4.*

Bell Pepper Stir-Fry

5 cloves of garlic, mashed
4 tablespoons chopped green onions
$2/3$ cup olive oil
5 cups assorted-color bell pepper strips
1 teaspoon ground black pepper
juice of 2 limes
$3/4$ teaspoon salt (if desired)
10 ounces pasta, any flavor
$1/4$ cup cilantro
$1/2$ cup diced feta cheese

Sauté garlic and green onions in olive oil in sauté pan for about 1 minute. Add bell peppers and cook for 4 minutes or until almost tender. Add black pepper, lime juice and salt. Boil pasta in a large pot until tender but still firm to the tooth. Drain. Serve vegetables over hot pasta sprinkled with cilantro and cheese. *Serves 4.*

Red Chile Pasta with Four-Cheese Sauce

Any and all of the chile-flavored pastas are delicious with this sauce.

1 pound Red Chile Linguine
1 tablespoon olive oil
1 cup whipping cream
$1/4$ cup shredded Swiss cheese
$1/3$ cup grated Parmesan cheese
$1/3$ cup shredded Monterey Jack cheese
$1/4$ cup shredded provolone cheese
salt and pepper to taste

Bring a large pot of water to a boil. Add linguine to boiling water, cook until al dente and drain. Toss with olive oil and place in a bowl. Keep warm.

In a large saucepan, heat cream just until it begins to simmer. Add the cheeses 1 at a time and stir until all are incorporated.

Toss pasta gently with sauce. Season with salt and pepper and serve at once. *Serves 6.*

Creamed Onion Sauce

There is no cream in this recipe; neither does one miss it. The onions, as they slowly cook, lose the sharp flavor and combine beautifully with the Parmesan cheese to produce a very good sauce. I have tried this sauce with all 9 flavored pastas we produce and have found it goes well with all of them.

1/2 stick butter or margarine
3 tablespoons olive oil
4 large onions, thinly sliced
3/4 cup dry white wine
3 cups chicken stock (vegetable broth may be substituted)
salt to taste
1 pound Jalapeño or Red Chile Pasta
freshly ground pepper to taste
1 1/4 cups freshly grated Parmesan cheese
1/4 cup thinly sliced green onions (whites and greens)

In a large skillet, melt the butter and mix in the olive oil. Add onions (not the green onions) and cook, covered, over medium heat for about 50 minutes, stirring occasionally. For the last 5 minutes, uncover and increase the heat to evaporate the moisture and brown the onions.

Mix the wine and the chicken stock together and add about 1 cup to the browned onions. Cook until most of the liquid is evaporated. Add the remaining liquid and boil until sauce is reduced by half and thickened.

Bring a large pot of water to a boil. Add salt if desired. Cook the pasta al dente and drain. Place the cooked pasta in a serving dish and add salt and pepper. Sprinkle with Parmesan cheese. Add sauce and toss. Top with sliced green onions. Serve at once! *Serves 6 to 8*.

pepper mill

Spinach Basil Garlic Linguine with Porcini and Cheese

1/2 ounce dry porcini mushrooms
2 cups warm broth or water
3 tablespoons butter
3 tablespoons olive oil
3 cloves of garlic, peeled and halved
1 pound Spinach Basil Garlic Linguine
1/2 cup (about 1/2 ounce) grated Parmesan cheese
2 tablespoons chopped parsley

Soak the porcini mushrooms in 2 cups warm broth or water for 20 minutes. Strain through a coffee filter and save the liquid. Rinse the mushrooms until they are free of sand.

In a medium saucepan, combine butter and oil. Over low heat, sauté the garlic until golden, stirring often. Discard the garlic and add the mushrooms and the strained liquid and cook over medium heat until all water is evaporated.

In a large pot, cook the pasta until al dente. Immediately drain and toss with mushrooms, cheese and parsley. Serve at once. *Serves 4 to 6.*

Butter Garlic Chile Pasta

1 teaspoon crushed fresh garlic
Butter to taste
10 ounces Jalapeño Chile Pasta, cooked, drained
4 ounces crumbled feta cheese

Sauté garlic in butter for 2 to 3 minutes. Toss with cooked pasta and sprinkle with feta cheese. *Serves 4.*

Hot Green Chile Pasta with Mushrooms, Peppers and Cream Sauce

10 ounces Green Chile Pasta
1 tablespoon olive oil
3 tablespoons butter
2 cloves of garlic
2 cups mushrooms, sliced
1 cup thinly sliced red bell peppers
1/4 cup green chiles
salt to taste
3/4 cup whipping cream
6 tablespoons grated Romano cheese
1 tablespoon parsley

Bring pasta to a boil in a large pot. Heat oil and butter in skillet. Add garlic and cook for 1 minute. Add mushrooms, bell peppers and chiles and cook for about 3 minutes. Add salt if desired. Add cream and 4 tablespoons of the Romano cheese and cook until thickened. Serve over hot cooked pasta sprinkled with 2 tablespoons Romano cheese and parsley. *Serves 4.*

Red Chile Pasta with Garlic and Oil

All pastas go well with this dish.

10 ounces Red Chile Pasta
4 large cloves of garlic, minced
1/4 cup (or less) olive oil
1/4 cup chopped parsley or cilantro
salt and freshly ground pepper to taste

Cook pasta in a large pot. Sauté garlic in oil in skillet until golden. Do not allow to brown. Add pasta and toss with herbs, salt and pepper. *Serves 4.*

❧ *If you like anchovies, this is a great way to have them with pasta. Just drain a 2-ounce can of anchovies, blotting with paper towel if needed, and sauté in a skillet with the garlic and oil.*

❧ *Add reconstituted dried tomato bits to the garlic and the oil or sauté a thinly sliced peperoncini with the garlic and the oil.*

Tomato Basil Garlic Pasta with Fresh Basil and Pine Nuts

This is definitely a summer dish, when fresh basil is luscious. Rinse it lightly with water and carefully paper-towel dry the leaves (the oil in the basil carries much of the flavor, so be careful not to remove it), stack them and cut into very thin ribbons. Romano cheese completes the dish.

1/2 pound Tomato Basil Garlic Linguine
2 cloves of garlic, crushed
1/4 cup extra-virgin olive oil
2 ounces pine nuts
3/4 cup fresh basil leaves, in ribbons
3 tablespoons white wine

Cook pasta in a large pot until al dente and drain. In a skillet, sauté garlic in oil for 1 minute. Add pine nuts and cook, stirring until lightly browned. Add basil leaves and wine; simmer for 1 minute. Add the pasta to skillet, toss with Romano cheese and serve immediately. *Serves 3 to 4.*

Tomato Basil Garlic Napolitano

1 medium onion, chopped
1 large carrot, finely chopped
2 cloves of garlic, minced
2 tablespoons olive oil
1/2 teaspoon ground pepper
1/2 cup broccoli florets
6 ripe Roma tomatoes, peeled, chopped
1 tablespoon chopped fresh basil (or 1 teaspoon dry)
salt to taste
10 ounces fresh Tomato Basil Garlic Pasta, cooked, drained
1 tablespoon grated Romano cheese

Sauté onion, carrot and garlic in olive oil in skillet for about 5 minutes. Add pepper, broccoli, tomatoes, basil and salt. Cook, stirring until vegetables are cooked but still crunchy (about 5 more minutes). Toss with cooked pasta; sprinkle with Romano cheese. *Serves 4.*

Olive Oil and Parmesan Basil Pasta

10 ounces Spinach Basil Garlic or Tomato Basil Garlic Pasta
3 tablespoons olive oil
1/4 cup freshly grated Parmesan cheese

Cook pasta in a large pot until tender but still firm to the tooth. Drain.
Heat olive oil and toss with pasta. Sprinkle with Parmesan cheese.
Serves 4.

Roasted Peppers Sauce

4 cloves of garlic, crushed
2 tablespoons vegetable or olive oil
2 each assorted-color chiles and bell peppers, roasted, thinly sliced
1/4 cup sliced peperoncini
1/2 cup olive oil
1/2 cup chopped parsley
1 cup grated Parmesan cheese
salt and pepper to taste

Sauté garlic in 2 tablespoons oil in skillet. Add peppers, peperoncini, 1/2
cup oil and parsley; cook for a few more minutes. Remove from heat and
allow to cool. Add Parmesan cheese, salt and pepper.

Use immediately over hot cooked pasta. Refrigerate for up to 6 hours but
allow to come to room temperature before using. Freeze for longer
storage. *Makes enough for 2 pounds of pasta.*

ଓଷ *In this sauce, the amount of oil used can be successfully cut in half with
not much loss of flavor. It can also be used as an appetizer served with
toasted thin slices of French bread, as a baked potato topping, or as a
burrito filling. Add meat or poultry if desired. This sauce freezes well.*

Oregano Cayenne Pasta with Cheese Sauce

1¹/₂ tablespoons butter
1¹/₂ tablespoons flour
1¹/₂ cups low-fat milk
1 cup shredded Swiss cheese
2 tablespoons grated Parmesan cheese
¹/₂ teaspoon dry mustard
salt and pepper to taste
10 ounces Oregano Cayenne Pasta
1 tablespoon olive oil

Melt butter in a saucepan. Remove from heat and add flour, stirring with wooden spoon. Return to heat; add milk slowly, stirring constantly. Cook until sauce is thickened, stirring constantly. Add cheeses and cook just until melted. Add dry mustard, salt and pepper. Cook pasta until al dente. Drain and toss with olive oil. Combine sauce with pasta. *Serves 4.*

ଔ *Compared with other cheese and cream sauces, this is not as high in fat, but it has a good flavor. If made ahead of time, reheat in double boiler. This sauce does a good job of "taming" the heat in the Oregano Cayenne Pasta.*

Gorgonzola and Walnut Cream Sauce

2 tablespoons butter
¹/₂ cup broken walnuts
1 cup cream
8 ounces Gorgonzola (or Stilton or bleu) cheese, crumbled
pinch of nutmeg
freshly ground pepper
salt (if desired)
10 ounces Black Pepper or Chile Pasta, cooked
grated Parmesan cheese
parsley

In a small skillet over medium heat, melt butter and stir in broken walnuts. Cook for about 3 minutes. Set aside. In a small saucepan, heat cream until hot (not boiling); stir in Gorgonzola cheese until melted, adding nutmeg, pepper and salt. Drain pasta and toss with sauce. Sprinkle with nuts, Parmesan cheese and parsley. *Serves 4.*

Jalapeño Linguine with Limas, Tomatoes and Mustard

1 tablespoon olive oil
2 tablespoons whole black mustard seeds
1/2 cup cilantro
1/4 cup thinly sliced green onions
1/2 cup broth
1 1/2 cups frozen lima beans
1 pound Roma tomatoes, seeded and cut lengthwise into strips
salt and pepper to taste
1 pound Jalapeño or Habanero Linguine
3 tablespoons olive oil
1/2 cup crumbled feta cheese

Heat the oil in a large skillet and add the black mustard seeds. Cook until they pop. Add cilantro and green onions and cook for 2 minutes. Add the broth and lima beans and cook, covered, until beans are soft. Add tomato strips, salt and pepper and and sauté for 1 minute.

Cook pasta in a large pot until al dente. Drain and toss with olive oil. Add sauce and serve immediately, sprinkled with feta cheese. *Serves 4 to 6.*

Pasta with Olives, Capers and Parmesan

1/4 cup extra-virgin olive oil
1/2 cup pimento-stuffed olives, sliced
1/4 cup black olives, sliced
1 tablespoon drained capers
1/2 teaspoon freshly ground pepper
10 ounces Tomato Basil Garlic, Spinach Basil Garlic or Herb-Speckled
    Pasta, cooked, drained
2 tablespoons chopped parsley
1/2 cup freshly grated Parmesan cheese

Heat the oil in a large skillet over medium heat for 2 minutes. Sauté the olives, capers and pepper. Toss with hot cooked pasta, parsley and Parmesan cheese. Serve at once. *Serves 4.*

Green Chile Mozzarella and Tomato Sauce

6 mild green chiles, roasted, peeled and diced
10 Roma tomatoes, peeled, seeded and diced
8 ounces mozzarella cheese, diced the same size as tomatoes
1/2 cup chopped fresh basil
1/2 cup piñon nuts
1/3 cup olive oil
1/4 cup freshly grated Parmesan cheese
salt and pepper to taste
10 ounces Tomato Basil or Spinach Basil Pasta, cooked

Mix all ingredients except pasta in a bowl. Toss with hot cooked pasta.

You can make the sauce ahead of time and refrigerate it, but remember to allow the sauce to come to room temperature before using it. *Serves 4 to 6.*

ᦝ *This uncooked sauce is one of my summertime favorites. Serve it on pasta or baked potato, hot or cold.*

ᦝ *You can substitute provolone cheese for the mozzarella cheese.*

ᦝ *If you like ham, 1 cup diced ham or 1/4 cup slivered prosciutto is a nice addition.*

Jalapeño Cream Pasta Sauce

1 large onion, diced
1/4 cup vegetable oil
1/2 cup pickled jalapeños
3 tablespoons flour
1 cup milk
1 1/4 cups whipping cream
3/4 cup grated Parmesan cheese
2 tablespoons chopped parsley
salt to taste
1 teaspoon freshly ground black pepper
1/8 teaspoon nutmeg
1 pound Jalapeño Linguine, cooked, drained

In a large saucepan, sauté onion in oil until tender. Add jalapeños and cook for 1 minute. Blend in flour, milk and cream, stirring constantly until smooth. Add cheese, parsley, salt, pepper and nutmeg. Cook for about 2 more minutes, stirring constantly. Remove from heat, and serve at once over hot cooked linguine. *Serves 6.*

ᙣ *If you have leftovers of this dish or if you want to double the recipe (so that you can have leftovers), you could serve it the next day as a soup. For each cup of sauce, add 3 cups well flavored chicken stock (see appendix). Bring to a boil and season with salt and pepper to taste. Serve sprinkled with chopped cilantro or green onions. Serves 4.*

ᙣ *Sauce goes well with chile-flavored pastas as well.*

Porcini Tomato Sauce

1/3 cup porcini mushrooms
1 cup boiling water
1 large onion, chopped
2 cloves of garlic, crushed
3 tablespoons olive oil
2 pounds canned Roma tomatoes, chopped
1/2 cup red wine
2 tablespoons chopped fresh basil (or 1 teaspoon dry)
salt and freshly ground pepper to taste
1 pound vegetable-flavor pasta, cooked, drained

Soak mushrooms in 1 cup boiling water for 30 minutes. Strain through a coffee filter, reserving liquid, and finely chop.

In a skillet, sauté onion, garlic and porcini mushrooms in olive oil for 5 minutes. Add tomatoes, reserved mushroom liquid, and wine. Simmer, uncovered, until thickened. Add basil, salt and pepper. Toss with hot cooked pasta (try Tomato Basil Garlic). **Serves 6.**

ᙣ *Pour sauce over cannelloni and bake topped with mozzarella cheese.*

ᙣ *The flavor of this sauce seems to improve overnight. I suggest making it the day before.*

ᙣ *This sauce can be served over cooked ravioli or tortellini.*

Herb-Speckled Pasta with Basil Garlic and Romano

Quick, easy and satisfying!

salt to taste
10 ounces Herb-Speckled Pasta
4 cloves of garlic, minced
1/4 cup olive oil
10 basil leaves, cut into strips
2 tablespoons sliced green onions
salt and freshly ground pepper to taste
4 ounces Romano cheese, shaved into curls with potato peeler

Bring a large pot of salted water to a boil. Cook pasta until tender but firm. Drain.

While pasta is cooking, sauté garlic in oil in a small skillet. Add basil, green onions, salt and pepper. Toss with hot cooked pasta and Romano cheese curls. *Serves 6.*

Green Chile and Cream Cheese Sauce

Very quick to make. Delicious.

2 tablespoons olive oil
4 green chiles, roasted, peeled and chopped
2 cloves of garlic, crushed
4 ounces cream cheese, cubed, at room temperature
1/3 cup milk
1/2 cup chopped cilantro
salt and pepper to taste
1/4 cup grated Parmesan cheese
10 ounces Red Chile Pasta
1 tablespoon olive oil

In a saucepan, heat 2 tablespoons olive oil and sauté chiles and garlic for 3 minutes. Add cream cheese, milk, half of the cilantro, salt and pepper.

Cook until cream cheese is melted and mixture is almost boiling, stirring constantly. Turn off heat; add remainder of cilantro and Parmesan cheese.

Cook pasta until tender but firm. Drain and toss with 1 tablespoon olive oil. Combine with sauce and serve at once. *Serves 4.*

ೞ *Use reduced-fat cream cheese if desired.*

Three-Mushroom Pasta Sauce

This sauce tastes even better the day after it is made.

1/3 ounce dry porcini mushrooms
1/3 ounce dry shiitake mushrooms
4 ounces fresh mushrooms, chopped
1 onion, thinly sliced
2 cloves of garlic, crushed
1/4 cup shredded carrot
1/4 cup olive oil
1/4 cup red wine
salt and freshly ground
    pepper to taste
2 pounds canned tomatoes,
    chopped
1 teaspoon thyme
1 pound Tomato Basil Garlic Pasta, cooked, drained

carrots

Soak each kind of dry mushrooms in 1 cup boiling water for 15 minutes. Strain through a coffee filter, reserving liquid; rinse and finely chop. Chop fresh mushrooms as well.

In a large skillet, sauté onion, garlic, carrot and fresh mushrooms in olive oil for five minutes. Add chopped reconstituted mushrooms, liquid from soaking, wine, salt and pepper. Cook for 2 more minutes. Add tomatoes and thyme. Simmer for about 10 minutes or until thickened. Toss with hot cooked pasta. Serve sprinkled with parsley and Parmesan cheese. *Serves 6 to 8.*

Porcini and Wine Cream Sauce

This sauce tastes very good with egg fettuccine and flavored pastas alike.

1 ounce dry porcini mushrooms
1 cup white wine
4 cloves of garlic, crushed
1/2 cup butter
3/4 cup cream
1/2 cup sliced green onions (whites and greens)
1 cup grated Parmesan cheese
12 ounces pasta (Black Pepper is my favorite) cooked, drained and
   tossed with 1 tablespoon butter

Soak mushrooms in wine in a bowl for 30 minutes. Strain through coffee filter and save liquid. Rinse porcini well and finely chop.

In saucepan, sauté garlic in 1/2 cup butter for 2 minutes. Add chopped porcini and wine. Cook for a few minutes or until reduced by half. Slowly add the cream, the green onions and the Parmesan cheese. Bring to a boil and stir, cooking until thick. Add the pasta, cook for another 3 minutes and serve at once. *Serves 4 to 6.*

ଔ *The rinsing of reconstituted dry mushrooms is done to remove bits of sand or growing medium still left on them.*

Green Chile and Romano Sauce

2 cups green chiles, roasted and cleaned, or canned chiles
1 cup pecans
1 cup grated Romano cheese
1/2 cup cilantro
4 cloves of garlic
1 cup olive oil
salt and freshly ground pepper
1 pound pasta (any flavor), cooked, drained

Coarsely chop green chiles and pecans in a food processor. Add cheese, cilantro and garlic, pulsing until chopped. Then using continuous speed, process while pouring oil over the top. Add salt and pepper. Serve immediately over hot cooked pasta. *Serves 6 to 8.*

- ○ Refrigerate for up to 6 hours. Freeze for longer storage.

- ○ Serve as a topping for baked potatoes, as an appetizer served with toasted thin slices of bread, stirred into soups, mixed with yogurt or mayonnaise as a salad dressing, on pizza instead of tomato sauce or over cooked poultry or seafood.

Dried and Fresh Tomato with Green Chile

3 green chiles, roasted, peeled and cleaned
5 marinated dried tomato halves, chopped
2 large ripe tomatoes, seeded and chopped
1/4 cup parsley leaves
1/3 cup walnuts
1/3 cup grated Parmesan cheese
1/3 cup green olive pieces
1/2 cup chopped basil leaves
1/2 cup extra-virgin olive oil
salt and pepper to taste
1 pound Jalapeño Pasta, cooked, drained

Place all ingredients except salt, pepper and pasta in bowl of food processor. Using the pulse mode, chop to a chunky sauce, or until smooth if desired. Add salt and pepper. Toss with hot cooked pasta. *Serves 6 to 8.*

- ○ For more texture, you could finely chop everything by hand instead of using the food processor.

- ○ Will go well with all other flavors of Adelina's pasta.

Rotini Napolitano

2 tablespoons olive oil
1 medium onion, chopped
1 large carrot, finely chopped
2 cloves of garlic, minced
1/2 teaspoon ground pepper
1/2 cup broccoli florets
6 ripe Roma tomatoes, peeled, chopped
1 tablespoon minced fresh basil (or 1 teaspoon dry)
salt to taste
10 ounces Tomato Basil Garlic Rotini, cooked, drained
1 tablespoon grated Romano cheese

Heat the oil in a skillet over medium heat. Sauté onion, carrot and garlic for approximately 5 minutes. Add pepper, broccoli, tomatoes, basil and salt. Cook for 5 minutes or until vegetables are cooked but still crunchy, stirring constantly.

Toss with hot cooked Tomato Basil Garlic Rotini and sprinkle with Romano cheese. *Serves 4.*

Oregano Cayenne Pasta with Garlic, Oil and Bread Crumbs

Extremely simple and a great, quick meal.

1/4 cup olive oil
2 large cloves of garlic, finely chopped
1/2 cup large bread crumbs (crumble French bread—no crust—and leave to dry)
2 green onions, thinly sliced
1/2 teaspoon freshly ground pepper
salt (if desired)
10 ounces Oregano Cayenne Pasta
1 tablespoon olive oil

Heat ¼ cup olive oil in a large skillet over medium heat. Sauté garlic until golden. Add bread crumbs and continue to cook until well toasted but not burnt. Add green onions, pepper and salt if desired. In a large pot, cook pasta, drain and toss with 1 tablespoon olive oil. Combine sauce with pasta and serve while hot. *Serves 4.*

附 *You can start the sauce as soon as you place the pasta in the boiling water. The sauce and pasta are usually ready together. Make sure your salad and whatever else you are serving is ready to go.*

附 *This dish can also be prepared and enjoyed with vegetable-flavor pastas.*

Linguine Romano

2 tablespoons olive oil
2 cloves of garlic, crushed
1 small onion, finely chopped
1 green bell pepper, finely chopped
2 stalks celery, finely chopped
5 ripe tomatoes, finely chopped
¼ cup red wine (optional)
salt, pepper and chile flakes to taste
10 ounces fresh Tomato or Spinach Basil Garlic Linguine

In a large skillet, heat oil. Add garlic, onion, green pepper and celery. Cook, covered, until vegetables are limp, but not soft. Add tomatoes, wine, salt, pepper and chile flakes. Cook, stirring at times, for 5 minutes. Uncover and cook for 5 more minutes. Adjust seasonings, adding more salt and pepper if needed.

Cook fresh pasta in a large pot of boiling water for 2 minutes or until tender but firm. When pasta has cooked, drain and immediately toss with prepared sauce. Serve at once. *Serves 4.*

附 *If you start with dry pasta, just cook it a few minutes longer until it is tender but firm.*

Fettuccine Florentine

1 1/2 cups Béchamel sauce
10 ounces Spinach Basil Garlic Fettuccine
1 tablespoon olive oil
1 1/2 cups low-fat ricotta cheese
1 (10-ounce) package frozen spinach, thawed and squeezed dry
1/2 cup grated Parmesan cheese
salt and pepper to taste
1/2 teaspoon Italian seasonings (basil, oregano, rosemary)

Preheat oven to 350 degrees.

Make Bechamel sauce (see following recipe).

Butter an oblong or square baking dish. Place fettuccine in 6 quarts boiling water in a large pot. Boil for 1 minute. Drain and toss with the olive oil.

Spread half of the fettuccine evenly in buttered baking dish. Spread ricotta cheese over noodles and spinach over cheese. Top with half of the Béchamel sauce. Sprinkle with Parmesan cheese, salt, pepper and Italian seasonings. Spread with another layer of fettuccine and pour the remaining Béchamel sauce over the top.

Bake for 20 to 25 minutes or until slightly brown on top. *Serves 4.*

Béchamel Sauce

1 1/2 tablespoons butter
1 1/2 tablespoons flour
1 1/2 cups low-fat milk
salt and pepper to taste

Melt butter in a small saucepan over low heat. Add flour and stir with wooden spoon for 2 to 3 minutes. Remove from heat. Add milk slowly while stirring until smooth. Return to heat and cook until thick, stirring constantly. Season with salt and pepper.

⅓ *You could add 1 cup freshly steamed asparagus, artichokes and/or 1/2 cup rinsed canned clams.*

Pasta and Asparagus

As an alternative to sauces, stir-fried vegetables and meats can also be served with flavored pastas. Because you can substitute vegetable or chicken stock for oil, there is a greater control over the amount of fat.

4 tablespoons olive oil*
4 cloves of garlic, thinly sliced
1 pound asparagus, steamed and sliced diagonally
salt to taste
1/2 teaspoon freshly ground pepper
10 ounces Habanero Tomato Basil Garlic Pasta, cooked, drained
1/2 cup grated Parmesan cheese

Heat oil over medium heat and sauté garlic for 1 minute. Add asparagus and stir-fry for about 2 minutes. (They should be cooked but still crispy.) Add salt and pepper. Mix with hot cooked pasta and toss with Parmesan cheese. Serve at once. *Serves 3 to 4.*

If you watch your fat intake, substitute up to 3 tablespoons of the oil with chicken or vegetable stock.

Peanut Butter Sauce

1 cup smooth peanut butter
1 cup light soy sauce
1 tablespoon crushed garlic
1/4 cup packed brown sugar
3 tablespoons vinegar
3 tablespoons water
2 green chiles, roasted, peeled and diced
1 teaspoon crushed red chiles
1/2 cup chopped cilantro
1 pound Black Pepper Pasta
3 green onions, sliced

Process all ingredients except the pasta and green onions in a food processor or beat with a wire whisk. Let stand for 10 minutes. Cook pasta until al dente and drain. Pour sauce over pasta and sprinkle with green onions. *Serves 6 to 8.*

Chile and Pasta Bake

2 tablespoons olive oil
2 tablespoons butter
4 to 6 green chiles, roasted, peeled and chopped
1 cup cooked peas
2 tablespoons flour
salt and pepper to taste
1 cup low-fat milk
1½ cups shredded Monterey Jack cheese
10 ounces Tomato Basil Garlic Pasta, cooked, drained

Preheat oven to 350 degrees.

Heat oil and butter in a saucepan over medium heat. Sauté chiles and peas for 2 or 3 minutes. Sprinkle in flour and stir for 2 minutes. Add salt and pepper. Lower heat and add milk a bit at a time until all is absorbed; cook until thick and smooth (may need a bit more milk or water). Turn off heat and add cheese. Stir to mix.

Butter a baking dish. In a large bowl, mix the hot cooked pasta and ½ of the chile sauce. Place mixture in baking dish and pour the rest of the sauce over it. Bake for 20 to 25 minutes until it is set, looks great and smells divine. Serve at once. *Serves 4.*

❃ *This dish also does well with a chile-flavored pasta.*

Tomato Brie on Pasta

1 pound Brie cheese
6 large ripe tomatoes
⅓ cup finely sliced basil leaves
2 cloves of garlic, crushed
3/4 cup olive oil
¼ cup grated Romano
½ teaspoon pepper
salt (if desired)
1 pound Black Pepper Pasta, cooked, drained

Dice Brie and place in a large bowl. Wash and chop tomatoes. Add tomatoes and all ingredients except pasta to the bowl and mix well.

Allow mixture to stand for 1 hour before serving. Serve over hot cooked pasta. *Serves 6*.

ᆼ *Make this sauce with vine-ripened tomatoes at the height of their sweetness. Home-grown tomatoes work best.*

ᆼ *Other flavors of Adelina's Pasta can be used. Red Chile, Jalapeño, Herb-Speckled, and Tomato Basil Garlic have all been tried with this sauce.*

ᆼ *This sauce also works well served over toasted French bread rounds as an appetizer.*

Green Chile Linguine with Creamed Puréed Spinach and Mushrooms

3 (10-ounce) packages frozen spinach
1 cup cream
3 tablespoons olive oil
4 tablespoons butter
1 pound mushrooms, thinly sliced
1/2 cup chopped green onions
1/2 teaspoon thyme leaves
salt to taste
1 teaspoon freshly ground pepper
1 pound Green Chile Linguine
1/4 cup coarsely grated Romano or Parmesan cheese

Preheat oven to 350 degrees and butter a large baking dish.

Place the spinach in a skillet and heat until it looks wilted and is a bright green color. Drain very well. Place in a food processor. Turn on machine and add the cream and oil slowly through the shoot.

In the meantime, heat a skillet and melt butter. Add the sliced mushrooms. Sauté in butter with green onions and thyme for 3 or 4 minutes. Add salt and pepper.

Boil the pasta in a large pot for just 4 minutes. Drain and place in buttered baking dish. Spoon the spinach purée over the pasta and top with the sautéed vegetables. Sprinkle with cheese. Bake, covered lightly with foil, for 20 minutes.

Bake, uncovered, for 10 minutes or until brown. Serve at once. *Serves 6*.

Jardinière Pasta Sauce

A celebration of summer. This recipe makes a large amount of sauce
(about 3 quarts) and freezes well.

1 cup vegetable oil
1 cup chopped onion
3 cloves of garlic, crushed
1 large eggplant, peeled, cubed
2 pounds Roma tomatoes
2 cups sliced mushrooms
oregano to taste
1 teaspoon salt (if desired)
$^1/_2$ teaspoon pepper
2 cups cubed zucchini
$^1/_2$ cup pimento strips
$^1/_2$ cup black olives, sliced
$^1/_2$ cup chopped fresh basil
salt and pepper to taste
2 cups grated Parmesan cheese

eggplant

In large pot, heat the oil and brown onion well (about 20 minutes over
medium heat). Add garlic and eggplant and cook for 10 more minutes.

Add tomatoes, mushrooms, oregano, salt and pepper and continue to
cook until about $^1/_2$ of the liquid has been evaporated. At this time add
zucchini, pimentos, olives and basil. Allow mixture to return to a boil and
cook for 5 more minutes. Add additional salt and pepper if necessary.
Turn off heat. Serve part of the sauce at once, sprinkled with Parmesan
cheese.

ᘓ *To freeze: when cool, mix in grated Parmesan cheese. Divide into desired
serving sizes in freezer containers. When ready to use, bring to room
temperature. Reheat in double boiler over hot water and serve over hot
cooked pasta. Serves tons of people.*

ᘓ *Very good served over baked potatoes or rice.*

ᘓ *Use as a filling for a tortilla to make a vegetable burrito.*

ᘓ *Pour over cannelloni or ravioli and bake.*

- Four cups of this sauce mixed with 4 cups chicken or vegetable broth becomes a hearty soup.

- If you live in New Mexico, you probably think this sauce is not complete without adding 6 to 8 freshly roasted and peeled green chiles cut into strips and added with zucchini. By all means do it! I certainly have!

Sautéed Vegetables with Oregano Cayenne Pasta and Bread Crumbs

1 pound Oregano Cayenne Linguine
1/4 cup plus 1 1/2 tablespoons olive oil
3 fresh vine-ripened tomatoes, diced
1 onion, thinly sliced
2 cloves of garlic, crushed
2 small yellow zucchini, diced
2 small green zucchini, diced
2 small eggplants, diced
1 green bell pepper, diced
2 tablespoons each chopped fresh basil, thyme and oregano
3 tablespoons balsamic vinegar

Topping
1 cup bread crumbs
1/2 cup grated Parmesan cheese
1/4 cup chopped fresh parsley

Cook linguine according to directions. Toss with 1 1/2 tablespoons of the olive oil. Keep warm. Heat the 1/4 cup olive oil over high heat. Sauté all vegetables until tender but crisp. Add herbs and balsamic vinegar. Toss with pasta. Mix all the ingredients for the topping together.

Divide pasta onto 6 plates. Top each serving with the bread crumb topping. Serve at once. *Serves 6.*

Tomato Sauce

My favorite tomato sauce. It is light and tasty.

4 ounces prosciutto ham, minced
2 tablespoons olive oil
1 tablespoon butter
4 medium white onions, chopped
2 tablespoons dry basil
4 cloves of garlic, minced
15 large ripe plum tomatoes, peeled and diced (or 2 pounds and 3 ounces
    canned Italian tomatoes put through a food mill or food processor)
1/2 teaspoon salt
freshly ground pepper
1 tablespoon chopped fresh parsley
1 pound Black Pepper or Spinach Pasta

In a saucepan over medium heat, sauté prosciutto in olive oil and butter
until crisp. Add onions, basil and garlic. Simmer for 3 minutes. Add
tomatoes and simmer for 20 minutes more, stirring frequently. Add salt
and pepper. (If still watery, increase heat and cook off any excess water.)
Add parsley. Boil the pasta in water in a large pot until tender but still
firm to the tooth. Drain and serve with sauce. *Serves 4 to 6.*

Asparagus and Mushroom Cream Sauce

1 pound asparagus, cut into 1-inch diagonals
3 tablespoons butter
1 tablespoon olive oil
2 cups chopped mushrooms
2 cloves of garlic, mashed
3/4 cup whipping cream
10 ounces pasta, any flavor
1/4 cup toasted piñon nuts
2 tablespoons grated Romano cheese
1 tablespoon chopped parsley

Steam asparagus until tender but crisp. In large skillet over medium heat, melt butter and add olive oil. Cook mushrooms for 4 minutes. Add garlic and sauté for 1 minute. Stir in cream. When boiling, add asparagus and turn off heat. Boil the pasta in water in a large pot until tender but still firm to the tooth. Drain and toss with sauce, piñon nuts, Romano cheese and parsley. *Serves 4.*

Like Peas in a Pasta

10 ounces Green Chile Rotini
salt to taste
1/2 cup cooked chick-peas
1/2 cup frozen tiny green peas, thawed
1/2 cup cooked black-eyed peas
4 tablespoons olive oil
1/2 cup olives
2 tablespoons capers
1/4 cup chopped pimentos
1/4 cup chopped peperoncini
1/2 teaspoon freshly ground
    black pepper
1 tablespoon chile flakes
1/2 cup grated Parmesan
    cheese

Boil the pasta in salted water in a large pot and cook until tender but firm. Drain, rinse, drain again and place in a mixing bowl. Add the peas. In a food processor, chop the olive oil, olives, capers, pimentos and peperoncini using the "pulse" button. Add black pepper and chile flakes. Mix well. Pour over pasta and peas and toss. Serve sprinkled with Parmesan cheese. *Serves 6.*

Parmesan and grater

Part Two

Chapter 7

Cold Pasta Dishes

Pasta salads are nothing new. The Japanese have been enjoying chilled noodles with crispy vegetables for many generations. The Chinese have contributed the soba (sesame-dressed noodles) and more recently, in southern Italy, hot summer days stimulated many cooks to create pasta dishes that could be served cold. However, it took the ingenuity of many creative American cooks to develop the variety of cold pasta dishes that are now part of the ever-evolving love affair with food. It is hard to imagine today a buffet table without two or more cold pasta dishes, or a potluck dinner without someone's favorite pasta salad.

It wasn't long ago that pasta salad meant boiled macaroni with mayonnaise and a few soggy vegetables mixed in for good measure. Today, the plethora of colors, textures, and flavors available by using fresh vegetables and cooked meats makes pasta salad one of the most versatile, satisfying, all-purpose dishes around.

In order to prepare a pasta salad that you can feel good about serving to guests (the true measure of food), there are certain rules you must follow. Although pasta salads have a high potential for greatness, the potential to create a most unappetizing mushy mess is just as great.

1. The first rule has to do with cooking the pasta. IT MUST BE COOKED AL DENTE (firm to the tooth). If you cook the pasta until it is soft, it will quickly absorb the dressing, swell, and become limp and mushy— not a happy sight, especially if prepared ahead of time.

2. Once the pasta is removed from the heat, it should be drained right away and rinsed with cold water to stop the cooking process. If it is not rinsed in cold water, it continues to cook and to get softer and softer and is on the road to becoming a mess.

3. As soon as it is rinsed and drained well, place in a bowl and toss with one tablespoon of the best light olive oil you can afford. (If you like the flavor of olive oil, that is. If not, use a good-quality salad oil.) The reasons for this are two-fold. The oil keeps the pasta from sticking and it coats the noodle with a thin film of oil that slows the dressing-absorption process. This way, you can taste the dressing better and the salad will last longer in the refrigerator.

4. Use the freshest vegetables available. They add color and texture. There is no way to make a good pasta salad with slimy peppers, wilted broccoli or zucchini, or dried-out garlic. Peas and baby Lima beans are the only vegetables that can successfully be used frozen (place in a colander and run hot water over them until soft; no cooking). Very crunchy vegetables like broccoli and cauliflowers should be blanched (see Preparing Foods for Eating) to retain crunchiness and enhance color. Always cut vegetables into small pieces.

5. Use a good-quality vegetable oil! You will taste what you put in. Where I grew up, green olive oil was always used with any kind of salads, potato, rice, lettuce, or vegetable.

6. Always serve pasta salad at room temperature. If made ahead of time, refrigerate, but bring out with enough time to reach the desired temperature. If you are worried about leaving certain cooked ingredients at room temperature (like cooked meats, poultry, or fish) keep them separate. That is, mix the pasta and the vegetables and keep the meat in a separate container. Add dressing to both. Bring pasta and vegetables to room temperature and add the meat, etc., just before serving. If the salad is made with a vinegar or lemon/lime dressing, a couple of hours out of the refrigerator will not cause much harm. Having grown up in a hot and humid environment, I don't take chances! I keep them separate and mix just before serving.

A pasta salad made and served following these rules should be delicious today, tomorrow, and even the next day.

Ham and Cheese Tomato Basil Garlic Pasta Salad

1 (10-ounce) package Tomato Basil Garlic Rotini, cooked according to
    directions
1 tablespoon olive oil
6 large Roma tomatoes, thinly sliced
6 fresh leaves of basil, chopped
4 ounces whole-milk mozzarella cheese, diced
4 ounces cooked ham, chopped
$1/2$ cup olive oil
2 cloves of garlic, crushed
3 tablespoons lime juice
$1/2$ teaspoon freshly ground pepper
salt to taste

Drain hot pasta and toss with 1 tablespoon olive oil. Place in bowl to cool.

Mix all other ingredients in a mixing bowl. When ready to serve, pour tomato mix over pasta. Toss gently. Serve at room temperature. *Serves 4.*

Red Chile Shells and Tuna Salad

1 (7-ounce) can white tuna chunks
$1/2$ cup thinly sliced water chestnuts
1 large green bell pepper, julienned
1 tablespoon thinly sliced chives
2 tablespoons finely chopped parsley
$1/3$ cup peanut oil
2 tablespoons red wine vinegar
1 tablespoon water
salt and freshly ground pepper
10 ounces Red Chile Pasta Shells
1 tablespoon peanut oil
$1/4$ cup dry-roasted peanuts

Drain the tuna and break into small chunks. Place in mixing bowl. Add water chestnuts, bell pepper, chives and parsley. In another bowl, whisk

1/3 cup oil, vinegar and water until well blended. Add salt and pepper. Mix into bowl containing tuna. Set aside on the counter.

Cook pasta al dente in water in a large pot; drain and rinse in cold water to stop the cooking process. Toss pasta with 1 tablespoon oil. When ready to serve, mix cooled pasta and tuna. Serve with peanuts sprinkled over. *Serves 4 to 6.*

Salad Mix Pasta with Salmon

2 small (1-inch diameter) zucchini, thinly sliced
2 small yellow squash, sliced
1 (7-ounce) can dry-pack smoked salmon
6 green onions (whites only), sliced lengthwise
1 cup blanched broccoli florets
1/4 cup sliced black olives
1/3 cup oil
2 tablespoons red wine vinegar
1 teaspoon dill weed
1 large clove of garlic, crushed
1/2 teaspoon freshly ground black pepper
1/2 teaspoon salt
10 ounces Salad Mix Rotini

Place zucchini and squash on 4 paper towels, wrap up and pat dry. Place in a mixing bowl. With a fork, separate salmon into bite-size pieces and add to zucchini/squash, along with green onions, blanched broccoli and sliced black olives.

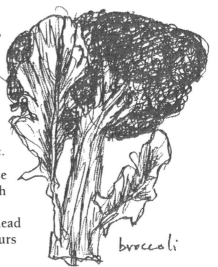

broccoli

Place next 6 ingredients in a jar with a lid and shake vigorously. Add to salmon mixture.

Cook rotini in a large pot until al dente. Rinse to cool quickly and shake out water. Mix with salmon and vegetables. Set aside at room temperature until ready to eat. If prepared ahead of time, refrigerate but bring out 1 1/2 to 2 hours before serving. *Serves 4 to 6.*

Tomato and Mozzarella Pasta Salad

One of my favorite pasta salads, it should not even be attempted if you don't have access to sun-ripened tomatoes and fresh basil. The sweet and tangy flavor of the tomato must carry the rest of the ingredients. There is no cooking of the sauce, so fresh, peak-of-flavor ingredients are a must.

6 large sun-ripened tomatoes
4 ounces whole milk mozzarella cheese, diced
1/2 cup chopped basil leaves
1 tablespoon finely sliced chives
2 large cloves of garlic, crushed
3/4 cup olive oil
2 tablespoons lime juice
1 teaspoon salt
a very generous amount of freshly milled black pepper
1/2 cup coarsely grated Parmesan cheese
1 pound Tomato Basil Garlic Linguine
1 tablespoon olive oil
salt to taste

Three hours before serving: Wash and pat dry tomatoes. Remove any blemish or dark spots. Cut into small pieces, placing tomatoes and then juice into a medium bowl. Add the rest of the ingredients (except the pasta and 1 tablespoon oil) and keep at room temperature.

Later: In a large pot of boiling water, cook linguine until tender but firm (not soft). Drain well, rinse with cold water, drain again and toss with 1 tablespoon oil. Set aside in a large mixing bowl.

Just before serving: Taste the sauce and correct seasonings, adding more pepper or salt if needed. Toss with cooled pasta and serve garnished with fresh basil leaves. *Serves 6 to 8.*

ଓ *This dish can also be served hot. Follow directions above, but omit the lime juice and mix with the pasta immediately after draining. The heat from the hot cooked pasta partially melts the mozzarella cheese, making it creamy. Serve with crusty bread and a lettuce salad.*

Pasta and Olive Salad

8 ounces Tomato Basil Garlic Rotini
8 ounces Green Chile Rotini
salt to taste
1 tablespoon olive oil
1 cup pitted green olives, sliced
1/2 cup pitted Greek olives, sliced
1 (4-ounce) jar diced pimentos
1/2 cup chopped peperoncini
3 cloves of garlic, crushed
3 tablespoons mini capers
2 tablespoons minced anchovies
1/2 cup olive oil
1/2 teaspoon dry oregano
1/2 teaspoon red chile flakes

Cook pasta together in plenty of lightly salted water in a large pot. Drain and rinse with cold water to cool quickly. Shake water out and mix with 1 tablespoon oil in a large bowl.

Combine all other ingredients in a small bowl. Mix with pasta and toss lightly. Set aside at room temperature, until ready to eat. Garnish with more Greek olives if desired. *Serves 6 to 8*.

cs *Make this heartier by adding 1/4 pound each of provolone cheese, hard salami and prosciutto ham, all julienned.*

capers

Green Chile Pasta Salad

10 ounces Green Chile Pasta
1 tablespoon olive oil
1 ripe avocado, peeled and chopped
1 small red onion, thinly sliced
1/3 cup chopped cilantro
1/2 cup chopped pecans
1/4 cup chopped pimentos
1/2 cup olive oil
1/4 cup lime juice
1 teaspoon crushed garlic
1/2 teaspoon fresh ground pepper
1/4 teaspoon crushed oregano leaves
salt to taste

Boil the pasta in a large pot until al dente. Rinse in cold water and toss with olive oil. Add avocado, onion, cilantro and pecans. Shake the remaining ingredients in a closed jar and toss with the pasta. Refrigerate for 2 hours. *Serves 4.*

℣ *Boiled shrimp makes a nice addition to this salad.*

Red Chile Pasta Salad

10 ounces Red Chile Pasta
1 tablespoon olive oil
3/4 pound fresh asparagus, steamed and sliced
1/4 cup each piñon nuts and sliced green onions (whites only)
1/2 cup olive oil
1/4 cup lemon juice
1 teaspoon crushed garlic
a pinch of cumin
salt to taste

Boil the pasta in a large pot until al dente. Rinse in cold water and toss with oil. Add asparagus, piñon nuts and green onions. Make marinade with remaining ingredients, pour over pasta, toss and refrigerate. *Serves 4.*

℣ *Sautéed scallops make a nice addition to this salad.*

Black Pepper Pasta Salad

10 ounces Black Pepper Rotini, cooked according to directions
1 tablespoon olive oil
1/2 cup each sliced red onion, chopped black olives and crumbled feta cheese
1/4 cup roasted, peeled and diced green chiles
2 Roma tomatoes, thinly sliced
1/2 cup extra-virgin olive oil
1 teaspoon dry oregano
2 tablespoons each lime juice, vinegar and water
1 tablespoon Dijon mustard
1/2 teaspoon salt and freshly ground pepper

Drain the pasta and toss with 1 tablespoon olive oil. Place in a large bowl to cool. Add onion, olives, cheese, chiles and tomatoes. Shake 1/2 cup oil with remaining ingredients in a jar. Toss gently with salad ingredients just before serving. *Serves 4 to 6.*

Smoked Salmon Pasta Salad

10 ounces Green Chile Rotini, cooked according to directions
1 tablespoon olive oil
1 (6-ounce) can dry-pack smoked salmon in large flakes
1/2 cup each sliced black olives and julienned zucchini
4 ounces provolone cheese, julienned
1/4 cup finely chopped parsley
3/4 cup light olive oil
1/4 cup wine vinegar
2 tablespoons water
1 clove of garlic
1 teaspoon Italian seasoning
freshly ground black pepper to taste

Salmon

Toss cooked pasta with 1 tablespoon olive oil and let cool. Add next 5 ingredients. Shake 3/4 cup olive oil with remaining ingredients in a jar. Toss with salad just before serving. *Serves 6.*

cs *Refrigerate leftovers of this dish, then microwave and serve as a hot dish. Other smoked seafood such as trout or scallops or smoked chicken or turkey also work well.*

Chile Pasta and Beans Salad

This is a winter salad. Although it is served at room temperature, the pasta will produce a satisfying warmth. It can be made in large amounts to serve a crowd.

2 large carrots, thinly sliced
1 cup small broccoli florets
1 pound Chile Pasta, cooked, drained and tossed with
    1 tablespoon olive oil
1 (8-ounce) can garbanzo beans, drained, rinsed
1 (10-ounce) can white beans, drained, rinsed
1/2 cup thinly sliced green onions
1/2 cup frozen peas, rinsed in hot water to thaw
1/2 cup chopped parsley

Vinaigrette

4 tablespoons lime juice
2 tablespoons balsamic vinegar
2 tablespoons water
1/2 cup olive oil
3 cloves of garlic, crushed
1 teaspoon salt
1 teaspoon freshly grated pepper

Blanch carrots and broccoli in a saucepan for 1 minute. Let cool. Mix with pasta, beans, green onions, peas and parsley in a large bowl.

For vinaigrette, place all ingredients in a jar and shake vigorously. Pour over salad mixture in bowl and toss gently. *Serves 10.*

⊳ *Other beans can also be used: black-eyed peas, lentils, black beans. If using canned beans, always rinse and drain them before adding them to the pasta.*

⊳ *Serve salad at room temperature. If made in advance, toss with vinaigrette just before serving.*

⊳ *Cooked meat or seafood can be added if desired.*

⊳ *The combination of pasta and legumes (beans) is an excellent source of complete protein.*

Chicken and Prosciutto Pasta Salad

10 ounces Spinach Basil Garlic Rotini, cooked, tossed with 1 tablespoon
  olive oil
1 chicken breast, sautéed whole, cooled and cut into strips
2 ounces prosciutto, cut into 1/4-inch strips
1 cup blanched small broccoli florets
1 cup cubed, blanched yellow squash
1 large almost-ripe tomato, diced

Dressing
2 tablespoons yogurt
juice of 1 lime
1 tablespoon vinegar
1/2 cup Basil Pesto (jarred or your own; see recipe page 33)
salt and pepper to taste
1/4 cup roasted piñon nuts

Combine rotini, chicken, prosciutto, broccoli, squash and tomato in a
large bowl. In a small bowl, whisk yogurt, lime, vinegar and pesto sauce.
Add salt and pepper. Mix salad ingredients with the dressing half an hour
before serving. Sprinkle with piñon nuts just before serving. *Serves 4 to 6.*

- ✂ *I make this recipe quite often using leftover chicken or turkey. The
  vegetables can be varied according to what you have.*

- ✂ *Leftovers, if any, should not be kept for more than 2 days in the
  refrigerator.*

- ✂ *This is a good dish to prepare in double or triple amount for a potluck or
  any other event where you are asked to bring a dish.*

Hot Chile Confetti Pasta Salad

Choose from your favorite vegetables for this salad—I like asparagus cut into 1-inch diagonals, frozen Italian green beans, broccoli and assorted colored bell peppers.

10 ounces Hot Chile Confetti Pasta
1 tablespoon olive oil
1/4 cup pine nuts or pecans
2 cups vegetables, blanched or boiled until tender-crisp

Dressing

1/2 cup olive oil
1/4 lime juice
2 tablespoons water
1 teaspoon garlic, crushed
1/2 teaspoon freshly ground pepper
salt to taste

Cook pasta in a large pot. Drain and add 1 tablespoon olive oil. Toss and set aside to cool. Mix pasta, nuts and vegetables in a large mixing bowl. Place all ingredients for dressing in a jar with a tight-fitting lid. Shake vigorously. Toss with pasta and vegetables. Serve at room temperature. *Serves 4.*

- *As in many other pasta salad recipes, the vegetables you use depend on what you like or what you have in your refrigerator or freezer. Blanching or boiling frozen vegetables will take less time than if you start out with fresh vegetables.*

- *If 1/2 cup oil looks like too much to you, reduce and substitute with broth, water or wine.*

- *In the wintertime I serve this salad hot. Just toss the vinaigrette with the hot cooked pasta.*

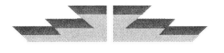

Part Two

Chapter 8

Vinaigrettes and Dressings

Vinaigrettes are the dressings of choice for flavored pasta salads. A light vinaigrette will bring out the flavor of the noodles, instead of masking it the way heavy mayonnaise- or cream-based dressings do. Another reason for using vinaigrette in all kinds of salads is that the amount of oil can easily be controlled without greatly affecting the flavor.

When I think of salads, I think of vinaigrettes. They complement the flavor of the ingredients in the salads, rather than overpower them. In the wintertime, vinaigrettes can be heated to serve with cooked vegetables.

In reading these recipes, you will notice, at times, I call for a raspberry, chile basil, thyme, etc., vinegar or oil. These flavored vinegars and oils are sold in my store and the recipes were developed with them. You could also use the many flavored oils and vinegars available on the market today or make your own using herbs, fruit, berries, spices, white vinegar (or olive oil) and wine.

Dried Tomato Vinaigrette

May be served hot or cold.

3 tablespoons vinegar
3 tablespoons balsamic vinegar
3/4 cup extra-virgin olive oil
2 cloves of garlic, crushed
salt to taste
1 teaspoon freshly ground black pepper
1/4 cup finely chopped mixture of basil, parsley and green onions
1/4 cup dried tomato bits

In a medium bowl, whisk vinegars, oil, garlic, salt and pepper. Add herb mixture and tomato bits. Allow to stand at room temperature for 1 hour. Refrigerate to keep, but serve at room temperature.

ଔ **Serving suggestion:** *this is a very versatile vinaigrette. It is very good on pasta or vegetables and on salads, including potato or rice salad.*

Lemon Dill Vinaigrette

juice of 2 lemons
3/4 cup vegetable oil
1/4 cup water
1/4 cup vinegar
2 tablespoons fresh dill weed or 1 tablespoon dry dill weed
1 tablespoon prepared mustard

Mix all ingredients in a cruet or jar and shake vigorously. Serve immediately.

ଔ **Serving suggestion:** *as a dressing for fresh green salads, as a dressing for vegetable salads, over sliced cucumbers or on chicken salad.*

Basil Vinaigrette

juice of 1 lemon
1 tablespoon Dijon mustard
1/4 cup basil vinegar
2 tablespoons water
1/4 cup minced fresh basil
2 cloves of garlic, crushed
2 tablespoons chopped parsley
3/4 cup olive oil
salt and pepper to taste

Whisk all ingredients in a mixing bowl until well blended. Refrigerate.

CB **Serving suggestion:** *good on pasta salads as well as green salads.*

Orange Raspberry Vinaigrette

Fresh spinach leaves, orange sections and sliced red onions are greatly enhanced by this dressing.

1/4 cup raspberry thyme vinegar
2 tablespoons water
1/2 teaspoon sugar or honey
1/4 cup orange juice
3/4 cup light olive oil
1 teaspoon freshly ground pepper
1 teaspoon salt

Mix all ingredients in a jar or cruet. Shake well. Keep refrigerated.

Red Pepper Vinaigrette

3 large red peppers, roasted, peeled and deveined
3 tablespoons balsamic vinegar
2 large cloves of garlic, crushed
1 tablespoon chopped parsley
1 tablespoon chopped fresh basil
2 teaspoons honey
1¹/₂ tablespoons olive oil
¹/₂ teaspoon freshly ground pepper
salt to taste

Process all ingredients in food processor. Use at room temperature right away. Refrigerate leftovers for up to 2 days, but bring to room temperature to serve.

ʘ *This dressing is good over pasta or spinach leaves, as a dressing for coleslaw or spooned over boiled new potatoes.*

Oregano Cayenne Vinaigrette

1 tablespoon oregano cayenne vinegar
4 tablespoons cider vinegar
3/4 cup Chile Seasoned olive oil
¹/₂ tablespoon oregano
juice of two limes
4 cloves of garlic, crushed
1 teaspoon freshly ground black pepper
salt to taste

Mix all ingredients in a jar. Shake. Refrigerate.

ʘ **Serving suggestion:** *this dressing is hot (chile hot). Use sparingly over cooked black-eyed peas or cooked black beans.*

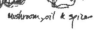

mushroom, oil & spices

Herb Vinaigrette

2 tablespoons Dijon mustard
2 tablespoons raspberry lime vinegar
1/2 teaspoon sugar
1/4 cup olive oil
1/4 cup chopped fresh herbs (basil, chives, parsley, etc.)
salt and freshly ground black pepper to taste

Shake all ingredients in a jar. Keep refrigerated but serve at room temperature.

Creamy Lime Mint Dressing

1/2 cup low-fat buttermilk
2 tablespoons chopped mint
2 tablespoons lime juice
1 teaspoon grated lime zest
1/2 teaspoon salt

Shake all ingredients together in a jar. Keep refrigerated.

∞ Serving suggestion: *this dressing is good over Spinach Basil Garlic Shells or cooked sliced carrots and peas.*

Cilantro Vinaigrette

1 cup packed cilantro leaves
1/2 cup chicken broth
2 tablespoons concentrated orange juice
1/2 teaspoon ground ginger
1/2 teaspoon ground cumin
1/2 teaspoon green or red chile powder
2 tablespoons olive oil
1 teaspoon salt

Place all ingredients in food processor. Process until smooth. Store in jar until ready to use. Serve at room temperature. If dressing is leftover, refrigerate for up to 2 days but bring to room temperature to serve.

Mango and Raspberry Vinaigrette

This vinaigrette does not contain any oil.

1 ripe mango, peeled, seeds removed, chopped
$1/4$ cup raspberry thyme vinegar
$1/4$ teaspoon chile pepper
1 teaspoon salt

Place all ingredients in blender. Remove from blender and pass through a strainer into a jar. Serve at room temperature.

ભ Serving suggestion: *good over spinach or green lettuce leaves, sliced red onions and mandarin orange sections.*

Blueberry and Mustard Vinaigrette

1 cup chicken broth, fat removed
$1/4$ cup blueberry lime vinegar
$1^1/2$ teaspoons grainy mustard
$1/2$ teaspoon dry oregano
$1/2$ teaspoon dry marjoram
2 tablespoons olive oil
1 teaspoon salt
freshly ground pepper

Process all ingredients in food processor. Refrigerate but bring to room temperature to serve.

ભ Serving suggestion: *serve over greens or pasta and vegetables.*

Strawberry Dressing

1 1/2 cups chopped, rinsed, cleaned strawberries
3 tablespoons raspberry thyme vinegar
1 tablespoon sugar
1 tablespoon thinly sliced green onions
2 tablespoons fresh tarragon
1/2 teaspoon cornstarch
1/2 cup freshly squeezed orange juice

Place berries in food processor and purée. Strain into measuring cup, adding vinegar and enough water to measure 1 cup. Empty into saucepan and add sugar, green onions and tarragon. Heat over medium heat. Mix cornstarch and orange juice and add to saucepan. Bring to a boil and simmer for 2 to 3 minutes. Allow to cool. When cool, check seasonings. If you prefer the dressing more tart, add a bit more raspberry thyme vinegar. *Makes 1 cup.*

 ∞ **Serving suggestion:** *this dressing is excellent on chicken salad or on salad greens. It has a sweet-and-tart flavor. It is beautiful in color too.*

Orange Raspberry Dressing

2 large oranges, washed
1 1/2 cups water
2 tablespoons sugar
1/4 cup raspberry thyme vinegar
1 teaspoon cornstarch
1 tablespoon cold water

With a potato peeler, take off strips of the orange skin, taking care not to include the white pith. Place strips on top of one another and with a sharp knife slice into thin shreds to measure 2 tablespoons. Place shreds in saucepan with a small amount of water, bring to a boil and drain. Cut and juice the oranges. Return the drained peel to saucepan and add 1 1/2 cups water, sugar, vinegar and orange juice. Bring to a boil. Add the cornstarch mixed with 1 tablespoon cold water. Simmer for 3 minutes. Cool. *Makes 1 1/2 cups.*

 ∞ **Serving suggestion:** *very good on spinach and mushroom salad or served over sliced cooked red potatoes.*

Part Two

Chapter 9

Fish and Seafood Pasta Dishes

With pasta being the national food of Italy and considering the vast coastal area surrounding that particular country, it should come as no surprise that so many combinations exist to make meals based on pasta and seafood. Using flavored pastas adds a new dimension to such combinations.

Because fish and seafood in general are sold on a tray wrapped with plastic film, it is very hard to verify if the fish is fresh. It is very important, indeed necessary, to cook only fresh or frozen fresh fish. Your nose will tell you right away if the fish is not fresh. If it is wrapped in plastic film, you can't smell it. If the supermarket has a seafood counter, most attendants refuse to let you smell the fish. Hah!

You could ask how fresh the fish is, but no reply will be as accurate as one good whiff. So this is what I do. I buy the fish, but before driving home, I unwrap the package and smell it. Then, if it smells "fishy" and strong, while I am still there, I take it back right away.

Refrigerate fresh fish as soon as you get home, and cook the same day if possible. Wash well before cooking, and when you cut it, make sure the cutting board is clean and dry.

Remember that seafood cooks very fast, so watch carefully and test often. If there are leftovers, refrigerate at once.

Green Chile Pasta and Shrimp in Warm Dressing

1 pound shrimp, shelled and deveined
juice of 1 lime
2 cloves of garlic, mashed
pinch of oregano
salt and freshly ground pepper
1 tablespoon butter
10 green onions, thinly sliced
6 canned or frozen artichoke hearts, diced
2 tablespoons lemon juice
2 tablespoons wine vinegar
$2/3$ cup extra-virgin olive oil
1 teaspoon prepared mustard
10 ounces Green Chile Pasta
6 fresh Roma tomatoes, seeded, chopped
12 black olives, sliced
$1/2$ pound full-milk mozzarella cheese, cubed
$1/2$ cup coriander leaves

Prepare shrimp and marinate in lime juice, garlic, oregano, salt and pepper for 1 hour. Drain and sauté in butter for 2 to 3 minutes or until firm. Set aside. Combine green onions and artichoke hearts in a bowl. Add lemon juice, vinegar, olive oil, mustard. Cook pasta al dente and drain. Immediately toss pasta with shrimp, tomatoes, olives and cheese. Pour dressing overpasta and toss along with coriander leaves. Serve at once.
Serves 6 or more.

leck

Mussels with Red Chile Pasta

4 pounds fresh mussels, scrubbed
$1/2$ cup white wine
4 shallots, chopped
$1/2$ cup minced parsley
cayenne pepper to taste
2 cups fish stock or 1 fish bouillon cube dissolved in 2 cups water
6 tablespoons butter
$1/3$ cup flour
1 cup sour cream
3 tablespoons chopped fresh basil
salt and pepper to taste
1 pound Red Chile Linguine, cut into 4-inch lengths, cooked, drained
1 tablespoon olive oil

Place mussels in large pot of water with wine, shallots, parsley and cayenne pepper. Cover and cook over high heat until mussels open (20 minutes). Discard any unopened mussels. Shell mussels; set aside. Strain liquid through a coffee filter. Add fish stock to the liquid. Over very low heat, melt 6 tablespoons butter in a large skillet. Sprinkle in flour and stir to make a paste. Gradually stir in mussel liquid until smooth. Cook for 3 minutes. Add sour cream and bring to a boil. Stir in the mussels, basil, salt and pepper and gently reheat. Toss pasta with olive oil. Divide among 6 plates. Top with sauce. Serve at once. *Serves 6.*

Green Chile Pasta with Shrimp Scampi

2 tablespoons butter
$1/2$ cup chopped onions
6 cloves of garlic, thinly sliced
2 tablespoons lime juice
salt and pepper to taste
1 pound shrimp, shelled and deveined
2 tablespoons each finely chopped parsley and green onions
2 tablespoons olive oil
2 tablespoons crushed red chile
1 teaspoon grated lemon zest
1 pound Green Chile Pasta, cooked

Melt butter in a large skillet over medium heat. Stir in onions, garlic, lime juice, salt and pepper. Cook for 5 minutes. Add shrimp and sauté for 3 minutes. Stir in parsley, green onions, olive oil, crushed red chile and lemon zest. Cook over high heat for 1 minute.

Drain pasta and add to skillet containing the sauce, stirring gently until mixed. Serve at once. *Serves 4 to 6.*

Habanero Pasta and Scallops

1 pound Habanero Pasta
3¹/₂ tablespoons olive oil
2 onions, finely chopped
3 cloves of garlic, crushed
2 tablespoons flour
1 (8-ounce) bottle clam juice
¹/₄ cup cream
³/₄ cup bay scallops, cleaned
salt, pepper and nutmeg to taste
¹/₄ cup fresh bread crumbs
¹/₄ cup grated Parmesan cheese
parsley as garnish

Cook Habanero pasta al dente (about 5 minutes). Drain and toss with ¹/₂ tablespoon of the olive oil. In skillet, heat 3 tablespoons olive oil and cook onions and garlic for 3 minutes. Add flour and cook for 2 more minutes, stirring constantly. Remove from heat.

In small mixing bowl, mix clam juice and cream. Slowly add to the onion mixture, stirring until all is incorporated and smooth. Return to heat; add scallops and simmer for 2 more minutes. Add salt, pepper and nutmeg to taste. Add cooked pasta and toss well until all is mixed. Transfer to a buttered baking dish. Mix fresh bread crumbs and Parmesan cheese; sprinkle over pasta. Broil for 5 minutes. Garnish with parsley before serving. *Serves 4 to 6.*

℣ *Shrimp may also be used in this dish.*

Herb-Speckled Pasta and Crab Bake

salt to taste
10 ounces dry Herb-Speckled Rigatoni or Rotini
1/2 teaspoon olive oil
1/2 pound of crab meat, picked clean
1 cup sour cream
1/2 cup ricotta cheese
10 ounces frozen peas, thawed
1/4 cup toasted almonds
3 tablespoons chopped green onions
3 cloves of garlic, crushed
1 teaspoon dill weed
freshly ground black pepper

Preheat oven to 350 degrees.

Bring a large pot of salted water to a boil. Cook the pasta al dente. Drain and toss with olive oil.

In large bowl, mix remaining ingredients with the just-cooked pasta. Pour into a buttered baking dish and bake for 30 minutes or until golden brown and bubbly. *Serves 4.*

Black Pepper Pasta with Anchovy Sauce

2 tablespoons olive oil
2 medium onions, finely chopped
2 cloves of garlic, crushed
2 tablespoons red chile flakes
2 (15-ounce) cans peeled whole tomatoes, chopped
1/3 cup sliced black olives
1 tablespoon dry oregano
1 tablespoon dry basil
1 (2-ounce) can anchovies, chopped
1/2 cup chopped parsley
salt and pepper to taste
10 ounces Black Pepper Pasta
2 tablespoons roasted pine nuts

In sauté pan, heat oil over medium heat and cook onions, garlic and red chile flakes for 5 minutes. Add tomatoes, olives, oregano and basil. Cook for 5 minutes. Add anchovies, parsley, salt and pepper.

Bring a large pot of water to a boil. Add salt if desired. Cook the pasta al dente; drain.

Pour sauce over Black Pepper Pasta and toss well. Sprinkle with pine nuts; serve immediately. *Serves 4.*

Green Chile Pasta with Salmon

Fast and easy. Delicious.

1/2 cup skim milk
3/4 cup chicken broth
8 ounces Neufchatel cheese, at room temperature, diced
2 cups fresh or frozen peas
1 teaspoon dill weed
1 tablespoon chopped parsley
salt and pepper to taste
10 ounces Green Chile Pasta
1 tablespoon olive oil
6 ounces dry pack smoked salmon

In a saucepan, slowly bring milk and broth to a boil. Lower temperature and add Neufchatel cheese. Cook, stirring until dissolved.

If peas are fresh, steam just until tender. If frozen, run hot water over them until thawed. Add peas, dill, parsley, salt and pepper to the sauce and cook over low heat until almost boiling.

Bring a large pot of water to a boil. Cook the pasta until tender but firm. Drain and toss with olive oil in a serving bowl.

Add fork-flaked salmon to the sauce and pour over just-cooked pasta. *Serves 4.*

⅓ *May also serve over Jalapeño or Black Pepper Pasta.*

Baked Rigatoni with Shrimp and Mushrooms

1/3 ounce dry porcini mushrooms
10 ounces Green Chile Rigatoni
1 tablespoon extra-virgin olive oil
2 tablespoons butter
1/4 cup flour
2 cups milk
nutmeg to taste
3 tablespoons olive oil
1/2 cup fresh button mushrooms
freshly milled pepper
1 pound shelled, deveined medium-size shrimp, chopped
4 ounces Swiss cheese, cut into strips
1 tablespoon chopped cilantro

Soak the dry porcini mushrooms in warm water for about 30 minutes. Drain; squeeze out water and chop finely.

Boil the rigatoni according to package directions. Drain and toss with 1 tablespoon of the olive oil in a mixing bowl.

Preheat oven to 350 degrees.

With butter, flour and milk make a Béchamel Sauce (see directions on page 62), sprinkle with nutmeg and cover to keep warm.

Place 3 tablespoons olive oil in a skillet. Sauté rehydrated porcini mushrooms and fresh mushrooms for 5 minutes. Add milled pepper liberally. Add shrimp and cook until shrimp turn pink (1 minute), stirring frequently. Remove from heat.

Pour Béchamel sauce and shrimp-mushroom sauté into the mixing bowl with the rigatoni. Add cheese and cilantro.

Pour into a lightly buttered baking dish and bake for 30 minutes. *Serves 4.*

೧೩ *With the same basic white sauce and mushrooms you could vary this recipe in many ways by substituting 1 cup cubed ham, leftover baked turkey or chicken or chopped tuna for the shrimp. For a vegetarian dish, add black-eyed peas or garbanzos.*

Rotini with Red Clam Sauce

1 teaspoon chopped garlic
olive oil
3 strips bacon, crisp-fried, crumbled
1/2 cup chopped onion
1 (14-ounce) can Italian tomatoes, chopped
2 (6-ounce) cans chopped clams
2 tablespoons chopped parsley
1/2 teaspoon dry basil
freshly milled pepper and salt to taste
10 ounces Herb-Speckled Rotini

rotini

In a medium skillet, sauté garlic in a small amount of olive oil until tender. Add bacon, onion, tomatoes, clams, parsley, basil, pepper and salt. Cook over medium heat until thickened, stirring constantly.

Boil the pasta in a large pot until tender but firm to the tooth. Drain. Immediately toss with sauce in bowl and serve. *Serves 4.*

Red Chile Fettuccine with Crab

Pretty to look at, delicious to eat, fast and easy to make.

10 ounces crab meat
4 tablespoons butter
1 1/2 teaspoons crushed garlic
1/2 cup cream
1/4 cup milk
1 teaspoon freshly milled pepper (rainbow colors if available)
1/2 cup freshly grated Parmesan cheese
1 pound Red Chile Fettuccine, cooked

In a skillet, sauté crab meat in 2 tablespoons of the butter for 2 minutes. Remove to a bowl. Add the remaining 2 tablespoons butter to skillet and sauté garlic to light golden. Add cream, milk and pepper. Bring almost to a boil. Add Parmesan cheese and crab meat. Heat just through.

Drain the fettuccine and add to cream sauce. Toss gently and serve at once. *Serves 6 to 8.*

Black Pepper Fettuccine with Anchovy-Caper Sauce

2 tablespoons olive oil
6 green onions, chopped
2 cloves of garlic, crushed
6 Roma tomatoes, finely chopped
1 (1-ounce) can anchovies, drained, chopped
2 tablespoons small capers
2 tablespoons chopped parsley
2 tablespoons chopped basil
$^1/_2$ cup sliced green olives
salt (if desired)
1 pound Black Pepper Fettuccine
1 tablespoon melted butter
$^1/_4$ cup grated Parmesan cheese
cherry tomatoes, sliced
basil leaves

Heat olive oil in skillet. Sauté green onions and garlic for 2 minutes. Add Roma tomatoes, anchovies and capers and simmer for 5 or 6 minutes. Add parsley and basil and sauté for 2 more minutes. Just before removing from heat, add sliced olives.

Bring a large pot of water to a boil. Add salt if desired. Cook the fettuccine just until tender. Drain and place in serving dish. Drizzle with melted butter and toss.

Add sauce, toss and serve sprinkled with Parmesan cheese and garnished with cherry tomatoes and basil leaves. *Serves 6 to 8.*

Linguine with White Clam Sauce

Any flavor of linguine from Herb-Speckled to Habanero will suit this sauce. It is just a matter of what flavor of pasta you feel like having today.

4 dozen cherrystone clams, scrubbed
1 cup white wine
1/2 cup olive oil
garlic to taste
2 cups clam juice
1/2 cup finely chopped parsley
1 teaspoon dry oregano
1 teaspoon freshly milled pepper
6 sun-dried tomato halves, cut into strips
1 pound linguine

Bring water to a boil in a large pot. Add clams and wine to the pot. Cover. Cook until shells open.* Cool and remove clams from shells. Strain liquid and set aside. Chop clams.

In deep skillet, heat all but 1 tablespoon of the oil and cook the garlic over low heat until tender. Increase heat and add reserved cooking liquid, clam juice, parsley, oregano, pepper and sun-dried tomatoes; simmer for 6 minutes.

Cook linguine until tender but firm. Drain and toss with remaining olive oil. Add clams to simmering sauce and heat briefly. Toss pasta and sauce and serve at once. *Serves 6.*

If some clams refuse to open, refuse to use them.

 og **Serving suggestion:** *Sourdough bread goes great with this dish.*

Green Chile Linguine with Garlic Shrimp

4 tablespoons olive oil
6 cloves of garlic, peeled and thinly sliced
1 tablespoon red chile flakes
1 pound shrimp, shelled and deveined
1 tablespoon fresh basil leaves, cut into strips
salt to taste
1/2 teaspoon freshly ground black pepper
1 pound Green Chile Linguine

Heat 3 tablespoons of the oil in a large skillet over medium heat. Add garlic and chile flakes and sauté for 2 minutes. Raise the heat to high and add the shrimp, stir-frying until it turns pink (about 3 minutes). Add basil, salt and pepper.

Bring 6 to 8 quarts of water to a boil. Add salt, if desired. Add the pasta and stir to make sure it does not clump and water circulates freely. As soon as it is tender but firm, drain and toss with the remaining olive oil. Add shrimp to linguine, toss and serve immediately. *Serves 4 to 6.*

Peppery Squid Linguine with Shrimp and Vegetables

1/4 cup olive oil
2 cloves of garlic, crushed
1 red bell pepper, diced
1 yellow zucchini, diced
1/4 cup sliced green onions
1/2 cup water chestnuts,
   rinsed, sliced
1 pound asparagus, boiled just until tender and sliced diagonally into
   1/2-inch thicknesses
1 1/2 pounds shrimp, shelled, deveined
salt and freshly ground pepper to taste
1/2 cup crumbled feta cheese
1 pound Peppery Squid Linguine
1 tablespoon olive oil

Heat ¹/₄ cup oil in a large skillet over medium heat. Add garlic and sauté for 2 minutes. Increase heat to high and add bell pepper, zucchini, green onions, water chestnuts and asparagus. Stir in shrimp. Cook for about 3 minutes. Add salt, pepper and feta cheese.

Bring a large pot of water to a boil. Add linguine to boiling water. Stir to make sure that it does not clump together. Water should circulate freely in and among the noodles. When tender but firm, drain and toss with 1 tablespoon olive oil and place in a large serving bowl. Add the sauce and toss gently. Serve sprinkled with feta cheese. *Serves 6 to 8.*

Bay Scallops Sauce

1 pound scallops
¹/₄ cup lime juice
8 green onions, finely sliced
4 tablespoons each olive oil and butter
²/₃ cup dry white wine
8 ounces clam juice
1 can Italian tomatoes, puréed
¹/₂ teaspoon freshly ground pepper
¹/₂ teaspoon fennel seeds
2 tablespoons butter
1 pound pasta, any flavor
1 tablespoon olive oil
¹/₂ cup chopped cilantro or parsley
¹/₂ tablespoon finely chopped lime zest
4 ounces feta cheese

Marinate scallops in lime juice for 30 minutes.

In a skillet, over medium heat, sauté green onions in 4 tablespoons oil and 4 tablespoons butter for 3 to 4 minutes. Add wine, clam juice, tomatoes, pepper and fennel seeds. Bring to a boil and simmer for about 10 minutes.

Drain scallops. Sauté in 2 tablespoons butter over medium-high heat for 3 minutes. Add to sauce just before serving.

Boil the pasta until tender but still firm to the tooth. Drain and toss with 1 tablespoon olive oil. Add sauce, cilantro, lime zest and feta cheese. *Serves 4.*

Part Two

Chapter 10

Chicken and Pasta Dishes

I could start this chapter by describing how I learned early in my cooking indoctrination the way to lure, trick, catch, kill, feather, clean and wash a chicken—any bird, really—to get it ready to cook. But it would not make any sense. Today it is possible to buy chickens and turkeys, and on rare occasions ducks, geese, and pheasants, in the supermarkets, ready to use.

Chicken, the most versatile of all meats, and pasta are very good to each other in hot or cold dishes. However, fresh poultry requires careful handling to avoid contamination. Whether you buy parts or whole birds make sure to wash it very well with water and pat dry with a paper towel (not a wash cloth) before handling. A clean knife and clean dry cutting board will reduce the risk of contamination with salmonella, the bacteria that causes salmonellosis, commonly known as food poisoning. Don't leave poultry out of the refrigerator for long periods of time.

If you marinade poultry for more than half an hour, do it in the refrigerator instead of at room temperature. Cook it until no pink juices come out when pierced with a fork. Once cooked, refrigerate leftovers as soon as possible.

Red Chile Pasta with Chicken and Black Olives

6 each chicken drumsticks and thighs, skinned
4 cloves of garlic, crushed
2 large onions, chopped
1/4 cup olive oil
1/2 cup red wine
1/2 cup water
1 cup frozen artichoke hearts
1 teaspoon each rosemary and thyme
1 cup black olives, sliced
1 bell pepper, deveined, seeded and diced
1 cup frozen peas
1/2 cup chopped parsley
salt and pepper to taste
1 pound Red Chile Pasta, cooked, drained and
    tossed with 1 tablespoon olive oil
1/2 cup crumbled feta cheese

Rinse and pat chicken dry. Rub with garlic.

In a large saucepan, sauté onions in olive oil for 10 minutes. Remove to bowl. In saucepan, brown chicken over medium heat. Reduce heat, return onions to pan and add wine, water, artichokes, rosemary and thyme. Cook, covered, for 20 minutes. Add olives, bell pepper, peas, half of the parsley, salt and pepper.

Cook, uncovered, for about 10 minutes to reduce the liquid by 1/2. Serve over hot cooked pasta sprinkled with remaining parsley and the feta cheese. *Serves 6 to 8.*

ᙜ *This sauce goes well with all Adelina's Pastas.*

ᙜ *Because there is more fat in brown chicken meats, you may want to substitute chicken breasts for drumsticks and thighs. If you do so, reduce cooking time by 10 minutes to keep the chicken from becoming dry.*

Red Chile Pasta with Chicken and Asparagus

10 ounces Red Chile Pasta
5 tablespoons olive oil
3/4 pound fresh asparagus, steamed and cut into 1-inch chunks
3 green onions, cut into thin diagonals
1 large clove of garlic, minced
1 sprig fresh thyme, chopped, or 1/4 teaspoon crushed dry thyme leaves
2 poached or roasted skinless chicken breasts, cut into cubes
salt to taste
1/4 teaspoon freshly ground pepper
1/4 cup freshly grated Parmesan cheese
juice of 1/2 lime

Cook pasta al dente. Drain. Heat oil in skillet and sauté vegetables, garlic and thyme for 1 minute. Add chicken, salt and pepper and heat through. Toss pasta with chicken mixture. Sprinkle with Parmesan cheese and lime juice. Serve at once. *Serves 6 or more.*

Tomato Basil Garlic Pasta with Chicken Scallopini

4 chicken thighs, skinned, boned and rinsed
flour for coating
2 tablespoons olive oil
1/2 cup white wine or chicken broth
1/2 cup whipping cream
1/2 teaspoon lemon zest
1/2 teaspoon crushed dry thyme
salt and pepper to taste
1/2 cup chopped cilantro
1 tablespoon lemon juice
10 ounces Tomato Basil Garlic Pasta, cooked, drained and tossed
    with 1 tablespoon olive oil

Pat dry chicken; pound thin between plastic wrap. Cut into 1-inch strips. Coat with flour and shake to remove excess.

In large pan, heat 2 tablespoons oil and cook chicken strips a few at a time for 1 1/2 minutes on each side. Keep chicken pieces in hot dish. Pour wine in the pan, bring to a boil and reduce the liquid to 1/2. Add cream, lemon zest and thyme; reduce for another 5 minutes. Add salt and pepper, chicken, cilantro and lemon juice; heat thoroughly. Serve over just-cooked pasta. *Serves 4.*

ଔ *Turkey may also be used.*

ଔ *If you don't want to use meat at all, peel and cut a large eggplant into strips and substitute for the chicken.*

Red Chile Linguine with Smoked Turkey

1/4 cup butter
1 onion, finely chopped
3/4 cup chicken broth
2 1/2 cups cubed smoked turkey or chicken
1 cup frozen peas, thawed
1 cup zucchini ribbons cut with potato peeler
1 cup yellow squash ribbons
2 tablespoons cornstarch
4 tablespoons water
salt and freshly ground pepper to taste
1 pound Red Chile Linguine, cooked, drained
1/2 cup grated Romano cheese

In a large skillet, heat the butter over medium heat. Stir in chopped onion and cook slowly until tender, for about 10 minutes. Add the chicken broth; allow it to come to a boil and simmer for 5 minutes. Stir in cubed turkey, peas, zucchini and squash and cook until heated through.

Mix cornstarch and water until smooth and add to sauce and turkey mixture. Add salt and pepper.

Add pasta to the skillet and toss. Cook for 1 or 2 minutes. Serve sprinkled with Romano cheese. *Serves 6 to 8.*

Chicken and Pasta in Tomato Sauce

Reminiscent of the chicken and rice I grew up with in the Caribbean, this has become a favorite at my family's table.

2 large cloves of garlic, crushed
1/2 teaspoon black pepper
1 tablespoon lime juice
6 tablespoons olive oil
2 pounds chicken thighs, skinned and deboned
1 large onion, chopped
4 tomatoes, peeled and chopped
3 tablespoons tomato paste
1 bay leaf
3 cups chicken broth
salt and pepper to taste
20 ounces Black Pepper Shells
10 olives
1 tablespoon capers

Prepare a marinade with garlic, pepper, lime juice and 2 tablespoons of the olive oil. Cut the chicken into bite-size pieces and toss with marinade. Refrigerate for 1 to 3 hours.

Lightly brown the chicken in remaining olive oil in a large skillet.

Remove chicken from the skillet. Add chopped onion to skillet and cook for 5 minutes. Add chicken, tomatoes, tomato paste, bay leaf, chicken broth, salt and pepper. Bring to a boil. Cover and simmer for 30 minutes.

Bring a large pot of salted water to a boil. Cook shells until just tender. Drain and add to chicken along with olives and capers. Cook for 3 minutes longer. Serve at once. *Serves 8.*

ଔ *I serve this in deep pasta bowls and eat it with a spoon. Sprinkle with Parmesan cheese if you want.*

ଔ *Leftovers do well reheated in the microwave.*

Chiles Rellēnos and Green Chile Pasta

6 green chiles, roasted, peeled
1 cup diced cooked chicken
1 cup shredded Monterey Jack cheese
1/4 cup chopped green onions
   (greens and whites)
1/2 teaspoon dry oregano
2 tablespoons chopped fresh cilantro
2 tablespoons chopped black olives
salt and pepper to taste
1 tablespoon olive oil
3 tablespoons butter
1 green chile, roasted, peeled, deveined and sliced
1 small onion, diced
3/4 cup cream
1/4 cup water
1/2 cup freshly grated Parmesan cheese
1 pound Green Chile Rotini, cooked, drained and tossed with olive oil

Preheat oven to 350 degrees. You can leave the stems on the chiles. Make a slit on the side to carefully remove the seeds and veins. Mix the next 6 ingredients and salt and pepper and fill the chiles with the mixture. Place in a buttered pan. Brush with oil and bake, covered, for 20 minutes.

Melt the butter in a saucepan and sauté the 1 green chile and onion for 5 minutes. Add cream and water and cook for another 5 minutes, stirring often. Turn off heat. Add Parmesan cheese and stir to mix.

Toss the cooked, drained and oil-tossed pasta with 1/4 cup of the cream sauce. Place in serving dish. Arrange the stuffed chiles on top and pour remaining sauce over all. Serve at once. *Serves 6.*

Ꮳ *The chicken may be roasted, boiled or even barbecued.*

Jalapeño (or Habanero) Linguine with Poached Chicken and Basil

2 quarts water
1/2 cup wine
2 chicken bouillon cubes
1 small onion, cut into quarters
1 carrot, cut into halves
1 celery stalk, cut into halves
4 large chicken breasts, boned, skinned
5 tablespoons olive oil
1/2 cup pine nuts
10 ounces frozen lima beans
1 pound Jalapeño or Habanero Linguine
salt to taste
12 large leaves fresh basil, cut into strips
1/2 cup grated Parmesan cheese

In a pan with a lid, place the water, wine, chicken bouillon, onion, carrot and celery. Bring to a boil. Carefully slip chicken into boiling liquid (liquid should cover chicken; if not, add more water). Lower the heat to where liquid stops boiling and small bubbles slowly rise to the top. Cover and poach for 12 to 15 minutes. (Make small cuts into chicken to make sure it has cooked through.) Remove chicken from liquid to cool slightly. Cut into bite-size pieces.

Heat oil in large skillet and brown pine nuts slightly. Add lima beans and cook until tender.

Cook linguine in plenty of salted water until tender but firm. Drain well and add to pine nuts and lima beans. Add chicken and basil leaves and toss well. Serve at once with grated Parmesan cheese. Garnish with fresh bay leaves if you have them. *Serves 4 to 6.*

ဢ *If chicken is poached well, it should be very tender and juicy with a good flavor. If intimidated by the poaching process, you may want to use leftover baked chicken or sautéed chicken breast. I have also used rotisserie chicken breasts, skins and bones removed.*

ဢ *You can also substitute cooked shrimp for the chicken.*

Green Chile Fettuccine with Chicken and Avocado

1^1/$_2$ pounds chicken tenders, cut into bite-size pieces
2 tablespoons lime juice
1 tablespoon olive oil
2 cloves of garlic, crushed
^{1}/$_2$ teaspoon oregano
^{1}/$_2$ teaspoon salt (if desired)
^{1}/$_2$ teaspoon freshly ground pepper
5 tablespoons olive oil
2 fresh or frozen green chiles, roasted, cleaned, diced
^{1}/$_2$ cup white wine
1 tablespoon lime juice
1 large avocado, peeled and diced
2 tablespoons chopped cilantro
1 pound Green Chile Fettuccine
^{1}/$_4$ cup grated Romano cheese

Rinse chicken and drain well. Place in mixing bowl.

In a small bowl, mix 2 tablespoons lime juice, 1 tablespoon olive oil, garlic, oregano, salt and pepper. Pour over chicken, toss and set aside for at least 30 minutes (if longer than 30 minutes, place in refrigerator).

Place 5 tablespoons olive oil in skillet over medium high heat. Brown chicken evenly. Add green chiles and wine. Cook, covered, for another 5 minutes.

Sprinkle 1 tablespoon lime juice over avocado and chopped cilantro.

Bring a large pot of water to a boil. Cook fettuccine until tender but firm. Drain and place in serving bowl. Pour chicken and avocado over fettuccine and toss lightly to mix. Serve sprinkled with Romano cheese.
Serves 4 to 6.

Spinach Basil Shells with Chicken and Dried Tomatoes

6 tablespoons olive oil
2 chicken breasts, skinned, boned and cut into strips
¼ cup wine
6 green onions, cut diagonally into 1-inch pieces
8 dried tomato halves, cut into strips
salt and freshly ground pepper to taste
10 ounces Spinach Basil Shells

In a large skillet, heat the olive oil and quickly brown chicken strips. Remove chicken from skillet and add wine to deglaze (soften and loosen brown bits that may have stuck to the pan). Add green onions, tomato strips, salt and pepper.

Cook shells in plenty of salted water until al dente. Drain and add to the skillet together with chicken. Toss well and serve at once. *Serves 4.*

ଔ *If you use marinated dried tomatoes, there is no need to cook for very long after you add them to the skillet. Marinated dried tomatoes are dried tomatoes that have been rehydrated and soaked in olive oil and basil. They are available in the supermarket or you can prepare your own.*

ଔ *If using dried tomatoes, you may want to rinse and microwave the tomatoes for 2 minutes before cutting, or pour boiling water over them and soak for 3 minutes to soften.*

salt and pepper

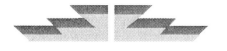

Part Two

Chapter 11

Pasta Dishes with Red Meat

The recipes in this chapter feature beef, pork, ham, lamb, and red meat in general but not as main ingredients. In keeping with the idea of this book, the meat is used in small amounts, mainly as a complement to flavor and texture, and usually in combination with pasta and vegetables.

When you buy fresh meat, refrigerate it immediately upon coming home if you plan to use it on the same or the next day. For longer storage it may be safer to freeze it, even though it will lose some of its texture and juiciness. Ham will last a few days longer in the refrigerator since it has preservatives. Rinse the fresh meat with water and pat it dry with a paper towel before slicing, cubing, or cutting in any other way, and make sure the cutting board is clean and dry. Since you can't rinse ground beef, make sure it looks good when you buy it (old ground beef looks dark and dry). Any leftover food containing meat should be refrigerated as soon as possible.

Green Chile Linguine with Meatballs

1¹/₂ pounds lean ground round
¹/₄ pound Italian sausage, cooked, drained, crumbled
1¹/₂ cups dried French bread crumbs
¹/₂ cup grated Parmesan cheese
1 small onion, finely chopped
3 cloves of garlic, crushed
2 tablespoons olive oil
1 teaspoon each dry oregano and dry basil
2 eggs or 2 egg whites and 1 egg yolk
¹/₄ cup each chopped parsley and ground fennel seeds

Mix all ingredients. Shape into meatballs and bake at 350 degrees for 20 minutes; drain.

Sauce

1 tablespoon olive oil
1 large onion, finely chopped
2 cloves of garlic, crushed
1 ounce dry porcini mushrooms, reconstituted, rinsed, chopped
³/₄ pound fresh mushrooms, chopped
2 (16-ounce) cans tomato purée
¹/₂ cup red wine
¹/₂ cup chopped fresh parsley
¹/₄ cup chopped fresh basil
1 teaspoon each black pepper and oregano
salt to taste
1 cup water
1 pound Green Chile Linguine, cooked, drained and tossed with
    1 tablespoon olive oil

In large saucepan, heat 1 tablespoon oil and cook onion, garlic and porcini mushrooms for 10 minutes. Add fresh mushrooms and cook for 5 minutes longer. Add meatballs, tomato purée, red wine, seasonings and water. Bring to a boil, cover and simmer for 30 minutes.

Serve pasta and sauce separately and allow each person to serve themselves the desired amount. *Serves 6 to 8.*

Habanero Pasta with Prosciutto and Swiss Cheese

Just like Alfredo sauces, this is high in fat. But it is delicious! This is one of those recipes that doesn't lend itself to substitutions. I feel better enjoying it once a year in all its glory, rather than tampering with it to make it less rich.

1/2 cup each cream and half-and-half
1/2 cup grated Swiss cheese
1/4 cup each grated Parmesan cheese and Romano cheese
1/4 pound prosciutto ham, chopped
1/4 cup olives
2 tablespoons chopped fresh basil
pepper to taste
10 ounces Habanero Pasta, cooked, drained

In a saucepan, mix cream and half-and-half. Heat, but do not allow to boil. Add cheeses and cook over low heat until sauce is smooth, stirring constantly. Add prosciutto, olives, basil and pepper. Serve at once over hot cooked pasta. *Serves 4.*

Green Chile Fettuccine Alfredo

1/2 cup butter
1 1/2 cups cream
1 cup artichoke hearts, cooked
1 cup grated Parmesan cheese
salt and freshly milled pepper to taste
1 pound Green Chile Fettuccine
1/8 teaspoon nutmeg

In a large skillet, melt the butter and add 1/2 cup of cream. Boil until thickened. Reduce heat. Add artichoke hearts, 1/2 cup cream, 1/4 cup Parmesan cheese, salt and pepper. Cook over low heat for 7 minutes.

Bring a large pot of water to boil. Add salt if desired. Cook fettuccine until al dente. Drain. Toss pasta with sauce, nutmeg and remaining cream and Parmesan cheese.

Chile Pasta and Black Bean Soup

2 tablespoons vegetable oil
1 large onion, finely chopped
3 cloves of garlic, crushed
3 stalks celery, diced
1 carrot, diced
3 fresh green chiles, roasted, peeled and diced
1 pound black beans, cleaned, washed and soaked overnight
1 pound tomatoes, peeled, diced
1 bay leaf
1/2 teaspoon dry thyme
1/2 teaspoon freshly ground pepper
10 cups water
1 cup uncooked Red or Green Chile Rotini
1 cup diced cooked ham

In a large stockpot, heat the oil over medium heat and sauté onion, garlic, celery, carrot and chiles for about 3 minutes. Add black beans, tomatoes, bay leaf, thyme, pepper and water. Bring to a boil and simmer for 3 hours or until the beans are tender. Purée 2 cups of the cooked beans and return them to the pot.

Add the pasta and ham and cook for 6 to 8 minutes. *Serves 6.*

ひ *If desired, a dollop of sour cream may be served on top.*

ひ *My favorite way of eating this dish is to top with a tablespoon of fruit vinegar just before serving.*

ひ *Vegetarians—leave the ham out.*

Black Pepper Pasta Stroganoff

The expression "a match made in heaven" reaches new heights when beef stroganoff is served over Black Pepper Fettuccine.

1/2 cup red wine
1/2 cup wine vinegar
3 pounds onions, finely chopped
2 cups cream
2 pounds beef fillet, cleaned and cut into julienne strips
1/4 cup vegetable oil
1 tablespoon Worcestershire sauce
1/4 cup chopped parsley
1 pound Black Pepper Fettuccine, cooked according
    to directions
salt and freshly ground pepper to taste
basil to taste

Pour wine and vinegar into a medium saucepan and bring to a boil. Add onions and cook over low heat until almost all liquid has been absorbed. Add 1 cup of the cream and cook to reduce liquid to half. Add the other cup of cream and cook until thickened, stirring constantly. Strain and keep warm.

In a skillet, sauté beef in oil over high heat a bit at a time just until browned, adding more oil if needed. Remove beef from skillet and keep warm. Add Worcestershire sauce to the skillet and bring to a boil. Add beef and parsley; again bring to a boil. Turn off heat. Stir in the cream sauce and adjust seasonings. Serve stroganoff over pasta. *Serves 6 to 8.*

Meat and Onion Pasta Sauce

3/4 pound ground round
1/4 pound ground pork
1/4 teaspoon each dry oregano and thyme
salt and pepper to taste
1 tablespoon butter
1 large onion, thinly sliced
1/2 cup cream
2 tablespoons balsamic vinegar
1 pound Black Pepper Linguine, cooked, drained
3/4 cup freshly shaved Parmesan cheese

Mix ground round and pork and season with oregano, thyme, salt and pepper. In a nonstick skillet, sauté mixture for 5 minutes or until browned and cooked through. Remove mixture to a dish and drain fat. Add butter and onion to skillet and cook until onion is soft. Add cream and balsamic vinegar. Cook to reduce the liquid by half. Adjust seasonings to taste and return the meat to the sauce. Heat through. Serve over hot cooked pasta and sprinkle generously with Parmesan cheese. *Serves 6.*

Black Pepper Linguine with Spiced Beef

East meets West—or is it Southwest meets East—whatever. This is a real favorite of "meatatarians."

1/2 pound beef tenderloin, fat removed
1/3 ounce dried shiitake mushrooms, soaked in boiling water for 20 minutes
6 tablespoons soy sauce
1 teaspoon hot sesame oil
3 tablespoons balsamic vinegar
3 large cloves of garlic, crushed
2 teaspoons freshly grated ginger
3 teaspoons vegetable oil
1 pound Black Pepper Linguine
1 bunch green onions, sliced diagonally
1/4 cup cilantro leaves (no stems)
2 tablespoons toasted sesame seeds
3 dried red chiles, seeds removed, thinly sliced

Rinse tenderloin and pat dry. Cut into julienne strips and place in a bowl. Julienne mushrooms and mix with tenderloin. In another bowl, make marinade with soy sauce, sesame oil, balsamic vinegar, garlic and ginger. Add about 2 tablespoons of the marinade to beef mixture. Marinate for 30 minutes.

Heat vegetable oil in skillet over high heat. Drain beef of marinade and quickly sauté for 1 minute. Remove from skillet and spread on dish to cool.

Bring a large pot of water to a boil. Cook linguine al dente. Drain and place in serving bowl. Toss with the remaining marinade.

Return beef to skillet, add green onions, cilantro, sesame seeds and red chiles; stir. Serve at once over noodles. *Serves 6 to 8.*

ꝏ *To toast sesame seeds, heat in dry skillet over low heat, stirring until golden brown.*

ꝏ *If you don't eat red meat, substitute julienned portobello mushrooms for the tenderloin. Process in the same way, but cook the mushrooms for 2 to 3 minutes longer.*

Spinach Basil Garlic Angel Hair and Ham

4 tablespoons butter
1 cup julienned cooked ham
1 egg yolk
$1/2$ cup cream
4 ounces freshly grated Romano cheese
$1/2$ cup sliced black olives
$1/4$ cup chopped parsley
10 ounces Spinach Basil Garlic Angel Hair Pasta

Melt the butter in a saucepan. Add ham and cook for 2 minutes. Mix the egg yolk and cream together. Add to the ham and heat without allowing mixture to boil. Add cheese, olives and parsley and keep warm.

Boil the pasta for no more than $1 1/2$ minutes. Drain and add to sauce, tossing gently. Serve at once. *Serves 4.*

Black Pepper Pasta with Sausage and Fresh Peppers

1/2 pound Italian sausage, pricked, cooked
2 tablespoons olive oil
2 medium onions, chopped
2 (15-ounce) cans peeled plum tomatoes or 3 pounds fresh
1 tablespoon crushed garlic
1/2 cup red table wine
1/2 cup water
1 each green and red bell pepper, cut into strips
1 teaspoon dry oregano
1 teaspoon dry thyme
1 teaspoon fennel seeds
salt and pepper to taste
2 tablespoons chopped fresh basil (or 1 tablespoon dry)
1 pound Black Pepper Linguine, cooked, drained
1/2 cup grated Parmesan cheese

Remove cooked sausage from pot and allow to cool, then slice. Drain the pot of all sausage fat and add olive oil and onions. Sauté for 5 minutes. Lower heat and cook, covered, for 10 minutes. Add tomatoes, garlic, wine, water, bell peppers, oregano, thyme, fennel seeds, salt, pepper and sliced sausages and cook for 20 minutes, adding fresh basil just before the end of the cooking time.

Add cooked pasta to the sauce and mix well. Serve at once, sprinkled with Parmesan cheese. *Serves 8.*

❈ *Ground chicken breasts, seasoned with lime juice, oregano and fennel seeds may substitute for the Italian sausage in this dish.*

❈ *This is a good sauce to make ahead and reheat.*

Part Two

Chapter 12

Polenta, Gnocchi and Couscous

Polenta

Many of our customers ask what polenta is and how to use it. Polenta, which is a traditional dish in many parts of Italy, is cornmeal cooked in water and a little salt until it is thick and smooth and doesn't taste raw anymore. To reach this point, it needs to be stirred constantly for 35 to 40 minutes, a job that gets harder as the polenta starts thickening. The proportions are 5^1/$_2$ cups water to 1^3/$_4$ cups cornmeal and 1 teaspoon salt.

Another way to make it without having to stir for such a long time is to bring the water to a boil, pour it into a stainless steel bowl and stir water in the same direction with a whisk. As a whirlpool forms, add the cornmeal slowly. Continue to stir, always in the same direction, until well blended. Then place bowl on top of a large pot of boiling water (bowl should not touch water), cover tightly with foil, and cook for about 1^1/$_4$ hours, stirring occasionally and always returning the foil cover.

To avoid this time-consuming process, you can use the precooked, dried polenta available commercially. Just follow the easy instructions.

Once it is cooked, what do you do?

Pour on a board, cool, slice into wedges and serve with butter or pour into a bread baking pan and allow it to cool. Unmold and slice.

To serve, there are many options.

Grilled: Brush slices of polenta on both sides with butter and grill until nice and brown. Serve with favorite spaghetti sauce and Parmesan cheese.

Pan Fried: Heat 2 tablespoons olive oil in a skillet and cook for 5 minutes on each side or until browned. Serve with slices of mozzarella cheese and a large dollop of hot salsa on top.

Layered Bake: Slice and layer in buttered dish. Alternate with a good ragout-type sauce and Parmesan cheese. Then bake for 45 minutes.

Gnocchi

Gnocchi are Italian dumplings. They can be made with semolina or flour and mashed potatoes and traditionally are served boiled, drained, and topped with a sauce. I have developed my own variation on the theme of gnocchi, which allows the flavor of chile to be incorporated in the dough.

Red Chile Gnocchi

You don't need a pasta machine to make these little morsels, although there are machines on the market that shape them. They can very successfully be shaped by hand, a great project for elementary-school-age children.

4 or 5 fresh red chiles, roasted
2 large eggs
2 cups unbleached flour
12 ounces ricotta cheese
2 tablespoons chopped cilantro
salt to taste
Parmesan cheese

potato

Clean roasted chiles and dry well with paper towels. Chop roughly in food processor with eggs. Turn processor on and off a few times until chiles are chopped into tiny pieces.

In a mixing bowl, place flour and egg/chile mixture, ricotta cheese and cilantro. Mix well until all is incorporated. Turn onto countertop and knead for 8 to 10 minutes or until smooth. Tear off chunks the size of an egg and roll between your hands and the counter to make a rope about 1/2 inch in diameter. Cut into 1-inch sections. With thumb, press the center to make an indentation. Place in plate. Repeat until all are prepared. Boil in plenty of salted water until the gnocchi rise to the surface; drain. Place in buttered dish; add a favorite sauce. Sprinkle with Parmesan cheese and bake at 400 degrees for approximately 20 minutes. *Serves 6 to 8.*

Couscous

Couscous is a type of pasta used in most countries around the Mediterranean Sea. Commercially available couscous is a semolina product (no cracked wheat), which has been made, steamed, and dried. This makes it easy to prepare since it only needs to be rehydrated.

At this point, I can only dream of couscous with chile already in it. Can you imagine red chile couscous with broiled bay scallops and shallots! I can't yet put chile in couscous, but I can put chiles on couscous.

Traditionally, couscous, which originated in North Africa, is steamed over the stew that is later served on it. In these recipes, boiling water is added to rehydrate and then it is mixed with the meat and/or sauce.

Red Chile Chicken and Couscous

6 boneless chicken thighs, cut into bite-size pieces
3 (or 6) dried red chiles, seeded and cut into thin strips
1/2 teaspoon each ground cloves, cinnamon, cardamom, cumin and turmeric
3/4 teaspoon salt
2 tablespoons vegetable oil
1 large onion, chopped
5 cloves of garlic, crushed
3 cups chicken broth
2 cups couscous
1/2 cup raisins or dried cranberries
2 cups boiling water
1/2 cup sliced almonds

Cut and rinse chicken pieces. Sprinkle with chiles and seasonings.

Heat the oil in a skillet and sauté onion and garlic for 3 minutes, stirring frequently. Add chicken and stir-fry for about 6 minutes. Add broth and bring to a boil. Cook for 2 minutes. Drain chicken and reserve liquid.

Place couscous and raisins in a container. Pour in 2 cups of boiling water; cover and set aside for 6 minutes.

Fluff the couscous and raisins and place in serving bowl. Top with the chicken and drizzle with the reserved liquid. Sprinkle with almonds. *Serves 6 to 8.*

Hot Couscous Primavera

2 cups couscous
2 cups boiling water
4 very small zucchini
4 small yellow squash
6 tablespoons vegetable oil
2 teaspoons freshly grated ginger
4 fresh green chiles, roasted, peeled and diced
6 cloves of garlic, minced
1 cup miniature carrots, cut lengthwise into halves
3 dried tomato halves, chopped
1/2 cup chopped green onions
1 cup small broccoli florets
3 cups chicken broth
1 tablespoon crushed red chile
salt and pepper to taste
1 tablespoon chopped parsley

Place couscous in a bowl. Pour in 2 cups of boiling water; cover bowl.

Cut zucchini and squash into 1/2-inch rounds.

Heat oil in a skillet. Sauté ginger, green chiles and garlic. Add carrots, dried tomatoes, green onions and broccoli. Stir-fry for 2 to 3 minutes. Add broth and bring to a boil. Add zucchini, squash and crushed red chile. Add salt and pepper to taste.

Fluff the couscous and place in serving bowl. Mix with vegetable mixture and serve sprinkled with parsley. *Serves 6 to 8.*

carrot

Couscous with Jalapeños, Salmon and Dill

2 cups couscous
2 cups boiling water
1 (6-ounce) can dry-pack smoked salmon
6 ounces heavy cream
2 tablespoons fresh dill
2 jalapeños, sliced paper thin
salt and pepper to taste

Place couscous and boiling water in a bowl; cover and set aside for 5 minutes. With a fork, flake the salmon into bite-size pieces.

In a small saucepan, heat the cream. Add dill, jalapeños, salt and pepper.

Fluff the couscous and place in serving bowl. Toss with salmon. Drizzle cream sauce over top. Serve at once. *Serves 6 to 8.*

Couscous and Eggplant Salad

2 cups boiling water
2 cups couscous
1 large eggplant, peeled, diced
1 large onion, sliced very thin
2 cups chicken broth
1 each red and green bell pepper, cut into thin strips
4 tomatoes, diced
3 tablespoons chopped parsley
6 tablespoons olive oil
2 tablespoons lemon juice
salt and pepper to taste

Pour 2 cups boiling water over couscous; cover and set aside for 5 minutes. Fluff and allow couscous to cool.

Place eggplant in a skillet with onion and chicken broth. Cook, covered, over medium heat until tender and liquid is evaporated. Place in bowl to cool.

Add pepper strips and remaining ingredients to eggplant mixture. Mix with cooled couscous. Serve in lettuce leaves. *Serves 6 to 8.*

Couscous with Cayenne Shrimp

4 cups chicken broth
2 cups couscous
1¹/₂ pounds shrimp, peeled and deveined
1 tablespoon cayenne pepper
4 cloves of garlic, crushed
4 tablespoons vegetable oil
1 cup frozen green peas, thawed
4 green onions, sliced diagonally into thin strips

Boil 2 cups of the chicken broth and pour over couscous; cover and set aside for 5 minutes.

Rinse and dry shrimp. Sprinkle shrimp with cayenne and crushed garlic. Heat oil in skillet and sauté shrimp, stirring often, just until cooked (2 to 3 minutes). Add remaining chicken broth and bring to a boil. Immediately remove shrimp to bowl. Cook until broth is reduced to ¹/₂, add peas and green onions and return shrimp to skillet, cooking for 1 more minute.

Fluff the couscous. Serve in bowl, topped with shrimp, peas and green onions. *Serves 6 to 8.*

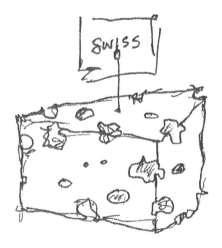

Appendix

How to Make Chicken, Beef, Fish and Vegetable Stock

I am a firm believer in stock as a base for many sauces. By starting with a good stock, you are well on your way to creating many delicious pasta sauces, soups and stews.

Chicken Stock

Make the stock with chicken backs and ribs, which can usually be found packed separately in the poultry section of the supermarket (just make sure they are washed well). I like to use a whole chicken (also washed well) since I can use the chicken meat in other dishes as well.

1 whole chicken or 4 pounds chicken backs and ribs
3 ribs celery
1 large onion, chopped
3 carrots, chopped
6 to 8 parsley sprigs
1 small bay leaf
salt and pepper

After removing the chicken from the package, rinse well to remove all sorts of "things" that sometimes accompany the bird, like pieces of feathers, dirt, blood, etc. Then rinse again. (I am trying to impress upon you how important it is to rinse poultry well.)

Place the now impeccably clean bird or bones in a large pot. Cover with water, add all other ingredients and bring to a boil over medium-high heat. Cover the pot, lower the heat to low and simmer for about 45 minutes. Strain the stock and use in the preparation of other dishes.

If you want a golden-color stock, brown the chicken first in 2 tablespoons vegetable oil. Then add the water and other ingredients.

Beef Stock

What would French onion soup be without a rich beef stock? It is not hard to prepare and is worth the time. While I prefer to use meat when making chicken stock, when it comes to beef stock, the bony parts alone will do well.

If you are friendly with the meat counter person at your supermarket you won't have any problem getting good bone and marrow cut in smaller pieces ready for your stock. If you aren't, don't worry. Just smile and ask nicely (they behave at times as if they don't want to do it).

Rinse the bones (shank, ribs, oxtail) well and brown in 2 tablespoons vegetable oil. Stir often to brown evenly. Browning will take about 30 minutes. If you have other things to do, place bones in a baking dish and brown in the oven for 1 hour. It takes longer, but you don't have to be there. When they are browned, remove to the pot and start removing all the wonderful juices that have stuck to the bottom. This is called deglazing. Scrape all into the soup pot. Add enough water to the browned bones to cover them by 2 inches. Add to this:

1 cup each chopped carrots, celery and onion
10 whole peppercorns
1 bay leaf
10 allspice berries
2 large cloves of garlic, bruised*

Bring to a boil over high heat, cover the pot, lower the heat and simmer for about 1 hour. Strain and save (freeze if necessary) to use as a base for soups, stews, sauces, etc.

*So, how do you bruise a clove of garlic? The same way you bruise anything. Just smack it hard! This will break the surface of the skin so that the flavor can come out easily. Place a knife sideways on the garlic and hit the flat part of the knife with the ball of your hand or press hard with the bottom of a thick glass or a clear glass bottle.

Fish Stock

You really need a good friend in the meat market to gather enough bones to make fish stock. Not because you will need so many, but because you will have to buy a lot of fish to gather enough bones. Bits of the fish flesh will add flavor too. When making fish stock, ask for bones of fish that are not oily, like haddock, sole, halibut, flounder, etc. However, if only oily fish are available, like salmon, make the stock the day before, refrigerate and the next day remove the layer of fat that has formed on the top.

Because of the delicate flavor of fish, you don't want any strong vegetables or spices that will mask the flavor. The bones, a small amount of salt, and a 1/4 teaspoon of your chosen herb (tarragon, thyme, or oregano) will be sufficient. No need to brown fish bones.

To make 6 to 8 cups of stock, you will need:

about 3 pounds fish bones
10 cups water
1 teaspoon salt (if desired)
1/4 teaspoon whole herbs (choose your favorite)

Rinse bones well, remove the gills and cut in pieces to fill your pan. Place bones in stockpot. Add water, salt if desired and herbs. Boil slowly for 30 minutes. Strain well.

Vegetable Stock

If I find myself in a situation where I really need stock and the only thing I can borrow from my neighbor is canned, I use it with some improvements.

2 cans stock
1/2 cup each chopped onion, carrot and celery
1 bay leaf
10 peppercorns

Place all in a saucepan and boil for 20 minutes. Strain well. Not perfect, but presentable.

Index

ANCHOVY
Black Pepper Fettuccine with
    Anchovy-Caper Sauce, 96
Black Pepper Pasta with
    Anchovy Sauce, 92
Parsley Anchovy Pesto, 34

ASPARAGUS
Asparagus and Mushroom
    Cream Sauce, 68
Pasta and Asparagus, 63
Peppery Squid Linguine with
    Shrimp and Vegetables, 98
Red Chile Pasta Salad, 76
Red Chile Pasta with Chicken
    and Asparagus, 102

BEEF
Beef Stock, 124
Black Pepper Linguine with
    Spiced Beef, 114
Black Pepper Pasta
    Stroganoff, 113
Green Chile Linguine with
    Meatballs, 26
Lasagna New Mexico, 26
Meat and Onion Pasta
    Sauce, 114
Meat Stuffing, 24

BLACK PEPPER PASTA
Black Pepper Fettuccine with
    Anchovy-Caper Sauce, 96
Black Pepper Linguine with
    Spiced Beef, 114
Black Pepper Pasta Salad, 77
Black Pepper Pasta
    Stroganoff, 113
Black Pepper Pasta with
    Anchovy Sauce, 92
Black Pepper Pasta with Sausage
    and Fresh Peppers, 116
Chicken and Pasta in Tomato
    Sauce, 104
Gorgonzola and Walnut Cream
    Sauce, 52
Meat and Onion Pasta
    Sauce, 114
Peanut Butter Sauce, 63
Porcini and Wine Cream
    Sauce, 58
Tomato Brie on Pasta, 64
Tomato Sauce, 68

CANNELLONI, 20
Green Chile Stuffing for
    Cannelloni, 21
Salmon and Leeks
    Cannelloni, 22
Scallops and Spinach
    Cannelloni, 23
Spinach and Crab Meat
    Cannelloni, 28

CAPERS
Black Pepper Fettuccine with
    Anchovy-Caper Sauce, 96
Pasta with Olives, Capers and
    Parmesan, 53

CHICKEN
Chicken and Pasta in Tomato
    Sauce, 104
Chicken and Prosciutto Pasta
    Salad, 79
Chicken Stock, 123
Chiles Rellenos and Green
    Chile Pasta, 105
Green Chile Fettuccine with
    Chicken and Avocado, 107
Jalapeño (or Habanero)
    Linguine with Poached
    Chicken and Basil, 106
Meat Stuffing, 24
Pesto and Poultry in Cold
    Pasta Dishes, 37
Red Chile Chicken and
    Couscous, 119
Red Chile Linguine with
    Smoked Turkey, 103
Red Chile Pasta with Chicken
    and Asparagus, 102
Red Chile Pasta with Chicken
    and Black Olives, 101
Spinach Basil Shells with
    Chicken and Dried
    Tomatoes, 108
Tomato Basil Garlic Pasta with
    Chicken Scallopini, 102

CHILE PASTA
Gorgonzola and Walnut Cream
    Sauce, 52

CLAMS
Linguine with White Clam
    Sauce, 97
Rotini with Red Clam
    Sauce, 95

Cold Pasta Dishes, 70

COUSCOUS, 119
Couscous and Eggplant
    Salad, 121
Couscous with Cayenne
    Shrimp, 122
Couscous with Jalapeños,
    Salmon and Dill, 121
Hot Couscous Primavera, 120
Red Chile Chicken and
    Couscous, 119

CRAB MEAT
Crab Meat and Shrimp
    Stuffing, 24
Herb-Speckled Pasta and Crab
    Bake, 92
Red Chile Fettuccine with
    Crab, 95
Spinach and Crab Meat
    Cannelloni, 28

FETTUCCINE
Black Pepper Fettuccine with
    Anchovy-Caper Sauce, 96
Black Pepper Pasta
    Stroganoff, 113
Fettuccine Florentine, 62

Green Chile Fettuccine
    Alfredo, 111
Green Chile Fettuccine with
    Chicken and Avocado, 107
Jalapeño Fettuccine with
    Roasted Garlic, 42
Red Chile Fettuccine with
    Crab, 95

GNOCCHI, 118
Red Chile Gnocchi, 118

GREEN CHILE PASTA
Baked Rigatoni with Shrimp and
    Mushrooms, 94
Chile Pasta and Black Bean
    Soup, 112
Chiles Rellenos and Green Chile
    Pasta, 105
Cream and Wine Primavera, 44
Green Chile Fettuccine
    Alfredo, 111
Green Chile Fettuccine with
    Chicken and Avocado, 107
Green Chile Linguine with
    Creamed Puréed Spinach
    and Mushrooms, 65
Green Chile Linguine with
    Garlic Shrimp, 98
Green Chile Linguine with
    Meatballs, 110
Green Chile Pasta and Shrimp
    in Warm Dressing, 89
Green Chile Pasta Salad, 76
Green Chile Pasta with Porcini
    Sauce, 42
Green Chile Pasta with
    Salmon, 93
Green Chile Pasta with Shrimp
    Scampi, 90
Hot Green Chile Pasta with
    Mushrooms, Peppers and
    Cream Sauce, 49
Like Peas in a Pasta, 69
Smoked Salmon Pasta
    Salad, 77

HAM
Chicken and Prosciutto Pasta
    Salad, 79
Chile Pasta and Black Bean
    Soup, 112
Habanero Pasta with Prosciutto
    and Swiss Cheese, 111
Ham and Cheese Tomato Basil
    Garlic Pasta Salad, 72
Ham and Tomato Basil
    Lasagna, 25
Spinach Basil Garlic Angel Hair
    and Ham, 115

HERB-SPECKLED PASTA
Herb-Speckled Pasta and Crab
    Bake, 92
Herb-Speckled Pasta with Basil
    Garlic and Romano, 56
Herb-Speckled Pasta with Garlic
    and Fresh Basil, 43
Olive Oil Primavera, 44

Pasta with Olives, Capers and
    Parmesan, 53
Rotini with Red Clam Sauce, 95

HOT CHILE CONFETTI PASTA
Hot Chile Confetti Pasta
    Salad, 80

JALAPENO PASTA
Butter Garlic Chile Pasta, 48
Creamed Onion Sauce, 47
Dried and Fresh Tomato with
    Green Chile, 59
Habanero Pasta and Scallops, 91
Habanero Pasta with Prosciutto
    and Swiss Cheese, 111
Jalapeño Cream Pasta Sauce, 54
Jalapeño Fettuccine with
    Roasted Garlic, 42
Jalapeño Linguine with Limas,
    Tomatoes and Mustard, 53
Jalapeño (or Habanero)
    Linguine with Poached
    Chicken and Basil, 106

LASAGNA, 18
Ham and Tomato Basil
    Lasagna, 25
Lasagna New Mexico, 26

LINGUINE
Black Pepper Linguine with
    Spiced Beef, 114
Black Pepper Pasta with Sausage
    and Fresh Peppers, 116
Green Chile Linguine with
    Creamed Puréed Spinach
    and Mushrooms, 65
Green Chile Linguine with
    Garlic Shrimp, 98
Green Chile Linguine with
    Meatballs, 110
Herb-Speckled Pasta with Garlic
    and Fresh Basil, 43
Jalapeño Cream Pasta Sauce, 54
Jalapeño Linguine with Limas,
    Tomatoes and Mustard, 53
Jalapeño (or Habanero)
    Linguine with Poached
    Chicken and Basil, 106
Linguine Romano, 61
Linguine with White Clam
    Sauce, 97
Meat and Onion Pasta
    Sauce, 114
Peppery Squid Linguine with
    Shrimp and Vegetables, 98
Red Chile Linguine with Smoked
    Turkey, 103
Red Chile Pasta with
    Four-Cheese Sauce, 46
Sautéed Vegetables with
    Oregano Cayenne Pasta
    and Bread Crumbs, 67
Spinach Basil Garlic Linguine
    with Porcini and
    Cheese, 48
Tomato and Mozzarella Pasta
    Salad, 74

Tomato Basil Garlic Pasta with
Fresh Basil and Pine
Nuts, 50

MUSHROOMS
Asparagus and Mushroom
Cream Sauce, 68
Baked Rigatoni with Shrimp
and Mushrooms, 94
Dill Yogurt and Mushroom
Sauce, 22
Green Chile Linguine with
Creamed Puréed Spinach
and Mushrooms, 65
Green Chile Linguine with
Meatballs, 110
Green Chile Pasta with Porcini
Sauce, 42
Hot Green Chile Pasta with
Mushrooms, Peppers and
Cream Sauce, 49
Pesto-Stuffed Mushrooms, 38
Porcini and Wine Cream
Sauce, 58
Porcini Tomato Sauce, 55
Sauce, 110
Spinach Basil Garlic Linguine
with Porcini and
Cheese, 48
Three-Mushroom Pasta
Sauce, 57

NAPOLITANO
Rotini Napolitano, 60
Tomato Basil Garlic
Napolitano, 50

OLIVES
Black Olives and Red Chile
Pesto, 34
Pasta and Olive Salad, 75
Pasta with Olives, Capers and
Parmesan, 53
Red Chile Pasta with Chicken
and Black Olives, 101

OREGANO CAYENNE PASTA
Oregano Cayenne Pasta with
Cheese Sauce, 52
Oregano Cayenne Pasta with
Garlic, Oil and Bread
Crumbs, 60
Sautéed Vegetables with
Oregano Cayenne Pasta
and Bread Crumbs, 67

PASTA PREPARATION
Basic Pasta Recipe, 13
Basic Recipe for Stuffed
Pasta, 18
Cold Pasta Dishes, 70
Cooking Techniques, 8
How to Cook Perfect Pasta, 15
Making and Cooking
Pasta, 12
Making and Cooking Stuffed
Pastas, 17
Making Flavored Pastas, 14
Pasta Has No Patience, 16

PEPPERS
Bell Pepper Stir-Fry, 46
Black Pepper Pasta with Sausage
and Fresh Peppers, 116

Hot Green Chile Pasta with
Mushrooms, Peppers and
Cream Sauce, 49
Peppers Pesto, 36
Red Pepper Vinaigrette, 84
Roasted Peppers Sauce, 51

PESTO
Basil Pesto, 33
Black Olives and Red Chile
Pesto, 34
Black Pepper Rigatoni and
Pesto, 38
Dried Tomato Pesto, 36
Green Chile and Romano Pesto
Sauce, 35
Other Uses for Pesto, 39
Parsley Anchovy Pesto, 34
Peppers Pesto, 36
Pesto and Poultry in Cold Pasta
Dishes, 37
Pesto and Uncooked Vegetable
and Herb Sauces, 32
Pesto-Stuffed Mushrooms, 38
Pistachio Basil Pesto, 35

**PLANNING MEALS WITH
PASTA, 29**
Your Pasta Shelf, 30

Polenta, 117

PORK
Black Pepper Pasta with Sausage
and Fresh Peppers, 116
Green Chile Linguine with
Meatballs, 110
Lasagna New Mexico, 26
Meat and Onion Pasta
Sauce, 114
Meat Stuffing, 24

PRIMAVERA
Cream and Wine Primavera, 44
Hot Couscous Primavera, 120
Olive Oil Primavera, 44
Very Low-Calorie Tomato Basil
Primavera, 45

RAVIOLI, 19
Green Chile and Herbs
Ravioli, 20

RED CHILE PASTA
Chile Pasta and Black Bean
Soup, 112
Cream and Wine Primavera, 44
Creamed Onion Sauce, 47
Green Chile and Cream Cheese
Sauce, 56
Mussels with Red Chile
Pasta, 90
Red Chile Fettuccine with
Crab, 95
Red Chile Linguine with
Smoked Turkey, 103
Red Chile Pasta and Cheese, 41
Red Chile Pasta Salad, 76
Red Chile Pasta with Chicken
and Asparagus, 102
Red Chile Pasta with Chicken
and Black Olives, 101
Red Chile Pasta with
Four-Cheese Sauce, 46

Red Chile Pasta with Garlic and
Oil, 49
Red Chile Pasta with
Vegetables, 41
Red Chile Shells and Tuna
Salad, 72

RIGATONI
Baked Rigatoni with Shrimp and
Mushrooms, 94
Black Pepper Rigatoni and
Pesto, 38

ROTINI
Black Pepper Pasta Salad, 77
Chicken and Prosciutto Pasta
Salad, 79
Chile Pasta and Black Bean
Soup, 112
Chiles Relleños and Green Chile
Pasta, 105
Ham and Cheese Tomato Basil
Garlic Pasta Salad, 72
Like Peas in a Pasta, 69
Pasta and Olive Salad, 75
Rotini Napolitano, 60
Rotini with Red Clam
Sauce, 95
Salad Mix Pasta with
Salmon, 73
Smoked Salmon Past
Salad, 77

SALADS
Black Pepper Pasta Salad, 77
Chicken and Prosciutto Pasta
Salad, 79
Chile Pasta and Beans Salad, 78
Couscous and Eggplant
Salad, 121
Green Chile Pasta Salad, 76
Ham and Cheese Tomato Basil
Garlic Pasta Salad, 72
Hot Chile Confetti Pasta
Salad, 80
Pasta and Olive Salad, 75
Red Chile Pasta Salad, 76
Red Chile Shells and Tuna
Salad, 72
Salad Mix Pasta with
Salmon, 73
Smoked Salmon Pasta Salad, 77
Tomato and Mozzarella Pasta
Salad, 74

SALADS, DRESSINGS
Basil Vinaigrette, 83
Blueberry and Mustard
Vinaigrette, 86
Cilantro Vinaigrette, 85
Creamy Lime Mint Dressing, 85
Dried Tomato Vinaigrette, 82
Herb Vinaigrette, 85
Lemon Dill Vinaigrette, 82
Mango and Raspberry
Vinaigrette, 86
Orange Raspberry Dressing, 87
Orange Raspberry
Vinaigrette, 83
Oregano Cayenne
Vinaigrette, 84
Red Pepper Vinaigrette, 84
Strawberry Dressing, 87
Vinaigrette, 78

SALMON
Couscous with Jalapeños,
Salmon and Dill, 121
Green Chile Pasta with
Salmon, 93
Salad Mix Pasta with
Salmon, 73
Salmon and Leeks Cannelloni, 22
Smoked Salmon Pasta
Salad, 77

SAUCES. See also Uncooked
Sauces
Asparagus and Mushroom
Cream Sauce, 68
Béchamel Sauce, 62
Bay Scallops Sauce, 99
Creamed Onion Sauce, 47
Dill Yogurt and Mushroom
Sauce, 22
Dried and Fresh Tomato with
Green Chile, 59
Gorgonzola and Walnut Cream
Sauce, 52
Green Chile and Cream Cheese
Sauce, 56
Green Chile and Romano
Sauce, 58
Green Chile Linguine with
Meatballs, 110
Green Chile Mozzarella and
Tomato Sauce, 54
Jalapeño Cream Pasta
Sauce, 54
Jardinière Pasta Sauce, 66
Meat and Onion Pasta
Sauce, 114
Meat Sauce, 26
Peanut Butter Sauce, 63
Porcini and Wine Cream
Sauce, 58
Porcini Tomato Sauce, 55
Roasted Peppers Sauce, 51
Sauce, 110
Three-Mushroom Pasta
Sauce, 57
Tomato Sauce, 68
White Sauce, 26

SCALLOPS
Bay Scallops Sauce, 99
Habanero Pasta and Scallops, 91
Scallops and Spinach
Cannelloni, 23

SEAFOOD
Baked Rigatoni with Shrimp and
Mushrooms, 94
Bay Scallops Sauce, 99
Black Pepper Fettuccine with
Anchovy-Caper Sauce, 96
Black Pepper Pasta with
Anchovy Sauce, 92
Couscous with Cayenne
Shrimp, 122
Couscous with Jalapeños,
Salmon and Dill, 121
Crab Meat and Shrimp
Stuffing, 24
Fish Stock, 125
Green Chile Linguine with
Garlic Shrimp, 98
Green Chile Pasta and Shrimp
in Warm Dressing, 89

Green Chile Pasta with
  Salmon, 93
Green Chile Pasta with Shrimp
  Scampi, 90
Habanero Pasta and Scallops, 91
Herb-Speckled Pasta and Crab
  Bake, 92
Linguine with White Clam
  Sauce, 97
Mussels with Red Chile
  Pasta, 90
Parsley Anchovy Pesto, 34
Peppery Squid Linguine with
  Shrimp and Vegetables, 98
Red Chile Fettuccine with
  Crab, 95
Red Chile Shells and Tuna
  Salad, 72
Rotini with Red Clam Sauce, 95
Salad Mix Pasta with
  Salmon, 73
Salmon and Leeks Cannelloni, 22
Scallops and Spinach
  Cannelloni, 23
Smoked Salmon Pasta Salad, 77
Spinach and Crab Meat
  Cannelloni, 28

SHRIMP
Baked Rigatoni with Shrimp
  and Mushrooms, 94
Couscous with Cayenne
  Shrimp, 122
Crab Meat and Shrimp
  Stuffing, 24
Green Chile Linguine with
  Garlic Shrimp, 98
Green Chile Pasta and Shrimp
  in Warm Dressing, 89
Green Chile Pasta with Shrimp
  Scampi, 90
Habanero Pasta and Scallops, 91
Peppery Squid Linguine with
  Shrimp and Vegetables, 98

SOUPS
Beef Stock, 124

Chicken Stock, 123
Chile Pasta and Black Bean
  Soup, 112
Fish Stock, 125
Vegetable Stock, 125

SPINACH
Fettuccine Florentine, 62
Green Chile Linguine with
  Creamed Puréed Spinach
  and Mushrooms, 65
Scallops and Spinach
  Cannelloni, 23
Spinach and Crab Meat
  Cannelloni, 28

SPINACH BASIL GARLIC PASTA
Chicken and Prosciutto Pasta
  Salad, 79
Fettuccine Florentine, 62
Linguine Romano, 61
Olive Oil and Parmesan Basil
  Pasta, 51
Pasta with Olives, Capers and
  Parmesan, 53
Spinach Basil Garlic Angel Hair
  and Ham, 115
Spinach Basil Garlic Linguine
  with Porcini and
  Cheese, 48

SPINACH BASIL PASTA
Green Chile Mozzarella and
  Tomato Sauce, 54
Spinach Basil Shells with
  Chicken and Dried
  Tomatoes, 108

SPINACH PASTA
Tomato Sauce, 68

STUFFED PASTA
Basic Recipe for Stuffed
  Pasta, 18
Cannelloni, 20
Crab Meat and Shrimp
  Stuffing, 24

Green Chile and Herbs
  Ravioli, 20
Green Chile Stuffing for
  Cannelloni, 21
Ham and Tomato Basil
  Lasagna, 25
Know Your Stuffed Pastas, 18
Lasagna, 18
Lasagna New Mexico, 26
Making and Cooking Stuffed
  Pastas, 17
Meat Stuffing, 24
Ravioli, 19
Ricotta, Green Chile and Fresh
  Herb Stuffing, 21
Salmon and Leeks Cannelloni, 22
Scallops and Spinach
  Cannelloni, 23
Spinach and Crab Meat
  Cannelloni, 28

TOMATO
Chicken and Pasta in Tomato
  Sauce, 104
Dried and Fresh Tomato with
  Green Chile, 59
Dried Tomato Pesto, 36
Dried Tomato Vinaigrette, 82
Green Chile Mozzarella and
  Tomato Sauce, 54
Ham and Tomato Basil
  Lasagna, 25
Jalapeño Linguine with Limas,
  Tomatoes and Mustard, 53
Porcini Tomato Sauce, 55
Spinach Basil Shells with
  Chicken and Dried
  Tomatoes, 108
Tomato and Mozzarella Pasta
  Salad, 74
Tomato Brie on Pasta, 64
Tomato Sauce, 68
Very Low-Calorie Tomato Basil
  Primavera, 45

TOMATO BASIL GARLIC PASTA
Chile and Pasta Bake, 64

Ham and Cheese Tomato Basil
  Garlic Pasta Salad, 72
Linguine Romano, 61
Olive Oil and Parmesan Basil
  Pasta, 51
Pasta and Asparagus, 63
Pasta and Olive Salad, 75
Pasta Putanesca, 45
Pasta with Olives, Capers and
  Parmesan, 53
Rotini Napolitano, 60
Three-Mushroom Pasta
  Sauce, 57
Tomato and Mozzarella Pasta
  Salad, 74
Tomato Basil Garlic
  Napolitano, 50
Tomato Basil Garlic Pasta with
  Chicken Scallopini, 102
Tomato Basil Garlic Pasta with
  Fresh Basil and Pine
  Nuts, 50
Very Low-Calorie Tomato Basil
  Primavera, 45

TOMATO BASIL PASTA
Green Chile Mozzarella and
  Tomato Sauce, 54

TURKEY
Red Chile Linguine with
  Smoked Turkey, 103

UNCOOKED SAUCES
Basil Pesto, 33
Black Olives and Red Chile
  Pesto, 34
Dried Tomato Pesto, 36
Green Chile and Romano Pesto
  Sauce, 35
Parsley Anchovy Pesto, 34
Peppers Pesto, 36
Pesto and Poultry in Cold Pasta
  Dishes, 37
Pesto and Uncooked Vegetable
  and Herb Sauces, 32
Pistachio Basil Pesto, 35

To order additional copies of this book

Send name(s), address(es), and $14.50 plus $3.00 for shipping and handling per book to:

Adelina's Products Inc.
P.O. Drawer L
Mesilla, New Mexico 88046

Check or Credit Card, please
Card type _____ Card # _____
Expiration Date _____

For a brochure of Adelina's Pastas and Gift Baskets:

Write to the above address; call (505) 527-1970 or (800) 687-3664;
fax (505) 527-0406; or better yet, come visit Adelina's Pasta Shop,
1800 Avenida de Mesilla, Las Cruces, New Mexico 88005